SKELETON KEYS

WORKPLACE HAUNTINGS

Dedication

Some say there is another existence after life.
They say, but cannot know.
This book is dedicated to Kurt, Arthur, and Ann,
members of our family who now know,
but cannot say.

Acknowledgments

Sincerest thanks to digital artist William Nadra for his interest in the success of this project and for his fine work as illustrator of this volume.

SKELETON KEYS

WORKPLACE HAUNTINGS

John Klann

4880 Lower Valley Road • Atglen, PA 19310

Other Schiffer Books on Related Subjects:

Eerie Encounters in Everyday Life: Angels, Aliens, Ghosts, and Haunts.
Thomas Freese. ISBN: 978-0-7643-4504-3.

Ghostly Beacons: Haunted Lighthouses of North America.
Therese Lanigan-Schmidt. ISBN: 978-0-7643-1114-7.

Ghosts in the Cemetery II: Farther Afield.
Stuart Schneider. ISBN: 978-0-7643-3590-7.

Haunted Highways and Ghostly Travelers.
Christopher E. Wolf. ISBN: 978-0-7643-3895-3.

Type set in Trade Gothic & Minion

ISBN: 978-0-7643-5208-9

Printed in China

Published by Schiffer Publishing, Ltd.
4880 Lower Valley Road
Atglen, PA 19310
Phone: (610) 593-1777; Fax: (610) 593-2002
E-mail: Info@schifferbooks.com
Web: www.schifferbooks.com

For our complete selection of fine books on this and related subjects, please visit our website at www.schifferbooks.com. You may also write for a free catalog.

Schiffer Publishing's titles are available at special discounts for bulk purchases for sales promotions or premiums. Special editions, including personalized covers, corporate imprints, and excerpts, can be created in large quantities for special needs. For more information, contact the publisher.

We are always looking for people to write books on new and related subjects. If you have an idea for a book, please contact us at proposals@schifferbooks.com.

Contents

Preface

Within the sphere of paranormal adherents there are assorted groups of people connected by shared experiences, expectations, and agendas. There are ghost hunters, people who seek paranormal encounters to further their knowledge of the phenomena, or to satisfy a need to identify with "the other side." There are storytellers who happily share their weird tales, taking pleasure in the retelling and the awe they often inspire. There are concealers, who keep such anecdotes buried out of sight for fear of ridicule, or to avoid resurrecting the emotions acknowledging them would stir up. There are even phasmophobiacs, a minor category of people who suffer from a fear of ghosts. Less studied is another group who suffer their paranormal confrontations, not because they move into a haunted house, and not because they seek thrills, but because their professional duties compel them to. Consider the curators of fabled historic sites, the realtors dealing with stigmatized houses abandoned by their owners, security personnel alone in darkened buildings all night, and you will begin to realize that there is a unique community of individuals occasionally forced to face the paranormal for no other reason than that it simply came with their territory.

The challenges that must produce, and how individuals cope with them, is a line of thought that, for me, had its seed planted by a personal experience, its scope broadened by hearing from kind people willing to share, and its evolution shaped by a temporary immersion into their world.

May the following recounting of my contributors' experiences and mine pique your interest in this unsung subset of resilient souls. Some have been assembled from interviews and long discussions. Others have been dramatized to provide context and enliven equally interesting but briefer communications with contributors who preferred anonymity.

All are true.

If the theme intrigues you, you will find material here worthy of your inspection. If you are one of these key holders yourself, you have found your peers.

Dear reader, I humbly present *Skeleton Keys*.

John Klann 2016

Introduction

Are there such things as ghosts?

If there are such things, what are they?

If ghosts exist, by what, if any, physical or spiritual laws are they governed?

All three of these compelling, centuries-old questions, can be answered with a single statement: We don't know.

So begins and ends the academic discussion of the facts surrounding what we commonly refer to as the supernatural. Beyond that humble admission we venture into a world of speculation, superstition, skepticism, and faith, four pillars built, unlike science, on foundations of fact-substitutes including emotion, sentiment, hope, fear, and every other intangible unit of measure humanity employs to make such abstract theories ring true or false.

This statement is not meant to imply that a serious discussion about a spirit world is not one worth having. Finding out where one stands on the question of the afterlife is one of the most basic of human philosophical pursuits. Perhaps no other belief can more profoundly affect one's approach to life and one's behavior as he journeys through it.

For those of us who lack the benefit of personal experiences with things paranormal, how we will come to a conclusion about the existence of alternative states will have more to do with our personal beliefs about what is probable, rather than any science regarding what is possible.

It is a fact that the scientific world can offer nothing in the way of knowledge of events after death apart from trivia regarding decomposition of the body. Science, as it exists today, can neither prove nor disprove the existence of a post-death world, therefore, science has no place at this table. No laws of physics, logic, biology, or psychology, can be cited for or against the case for a plane of existence different from the one we comprehend through our senses while alive on Earth. Technology has evolved to offer clues, but no

conclusions. What is left to us are the verbal accounts of others and our ability to accept that reality is relative.

According to the dictionary, "supernatural" refers to things outside nature and therefore not governed by the laws of nature. I would like to challenge the distinction between the concepts of "natural" and "supernatural." If no altered state of a human being after corporal death exists, than ghosts are not supernatural, they are fiction. If they do exist, they are, they must be, natural. Consider that in the past, people applied the label of supernatural to forces of nature, heavenly bodies, to other people, and to things, until those subjects were discovered to be parts of the natural world that the observers, at first, simply didn't understand. Accounts, like the ones that follow, of individuals from opposing states of existence interacting from time to time, if true, lend support to the idea that what we term paranormal phenomena is actually a normal, if hardly understood, part of the natural world.

This vexing gap in humanity's understanding has possibly intrigued everyone who has ever existed to some extent, and definitely fascinated others, like myself, for large parts of their lives. To inch closer to the truth, I have collected people's "ghost stories" in an attempt to gain insight into what might, or might not, be part of this other side we seem unable to make up our minds about.

American naturalist John Muir is quoted as having said, "When one tugs at a single thing in nature, he finds it attached to the rest of the world."

I wonder how big that "rest of the world" really is. If you also wonder, then read on, for we are seekers on the same path, birds of a feather, we are, dare I say it, kindred spirits.

1

Footsteps Cross the Empty Room

The idea that there are those among us who have their brushes with the stranger side of life, not because they are particularly interested in doing so, but because it has, unfortunately for them, become part of their daily routine, first presented itself to me when the job of finding a new place to live paired me with a real estate agent whose full name I will withhold, and whose face, for reasons that will become evident in the following account, I shall never forget. Before and during the time I spent with this gentleman, walking through empty old houses was something one did in a business-like way, paying attention to details related to the soundness of plaster, the condition of carpets, and any noticeable cupping of the shingles on roofs. There were no background concerns about stigmas, legends, or presences. Not yet.

In 2001, my family and I were living on Long Island, New York, but we wanted to live in Lancaster County, Pennsylvania. The rural locale, to which we retreated twice yearly, and some years more, was an inviting, homey respite from the demands of a life dominated by long hours of commuting and the maintenance of our aging, miniature home on a stretch of road where the traffic never ceased rattling our windows and made impossible the idea of peace and quiet for all time. We were not town people, and after years of visiting the Lancaster area as tourists seeking a getaway, we finally asked ourselves why it was that we were spending our lives in a place where we felt like we were somehow in the way, and only passing through the place that felt like home. The decision was a bold one, and it carried with it the potential for serious consequences, but in the end it was easy to make because it was right—we would leave everything and everyone we had ever known, and, without family, prospect of employment, or much of a plan, we would relocate to where we believed we and our young son would find the life that suited us best.

House hunting can be a strange journey, a mixture of joy and anticipation, peppered with fatigue, fear, and deep, resolve-crushing disappointments. For our Pennsylvania quest, our guide through the rabbit hole was Tom, a wiry, well-dressed gentleman, a few years our senior, who seemed to hear us when we ran through our criteria, but more often than not, took us to tour houses that were nothing short of the exact opposite of what we had told him we were looking for. I suppose all realtors do this covering of the bases on the assumption that clients might think they know what they want, but, when better versed on the alternatives, might find they have a penchant for small, weirdly shaped stuccoed buildings after all.

So it was that every weekend we would make our trip out to the country, live in a hotel for a night and a day, and tour houses, plain to grand, that people had either grown tired of, or, like us, needed to move on from. We established with Tom that we preferred older homes to new ones, in fact the older the better. In the market of the day, inventory was short and selections came from the periphery of our criteria. We were introduced to farmhouses that were just a bit too bare bones, and offered tidy quasi-Victorians that had interior features but little to no property. We were tempted by an old 1901 restoration that, unfortunately, shared a border with the state's largest, stadium lighted, auto auction, and were even tempted by a three-story mansion whose aged occupant was willing to sell, as long as we agreed to share the building with him until such time as he should pass from this world to the next. Over time, however, and with Tom's help, we finally did find our new home and made the move. One journey was over, but along the way another had presented its first, disturbing sign.

It was during week six or seven of the trial that was our house hunt, that my wife and I, leaving our son back home with grandparents for a hiatus, were taken to a secluded development by our agent to take a look at a large two-story split level home somewhere in Lancaster County. From the outside, the house was mildly impressive by virtue of its size and relative newness, but since all I did those days was look at houses, it read as just another throwaway and I determined to make the visit as short as possible. I was prepared to be bored.

Tom used his master key to get the house key out of the lock box and opened the door. Inside we found the house neat and well appointed. The style of the interiors were dated, late '70s to early '80s it seemed to me. I took note of the layout as Tom started his pitch. As always, we would make our way from the front to the back and from the bottom to the top, all the while opening every closet door, every cabinet, and most of the drawers. Tom showed us the coat closet, the dining room off the hall, the hall, the living room. The three of us went slowly from room to room, my wife and I measuring with our eyes, envisioning how our tiny furniture would look in these upgraded settings, Tom extolling the virtues of Corian and ceramic tile. Gradually, I started to become aware of a feeling. There was something about this experience that was subtly different from the others. There seemed to be, for want of a better word, an attitude about the house. As I stated before, all I did in those days was inspect other people's houses, but now I had the unusual notion that, perhaps, impossibly, this one was inspecting me.

Pushing the sensation aside, I returned to the work of trying to pry any value I could from the remainder of the house tour. We saw the family room, the kitchen, the yard outside the sliding glass door. The rooms were unremarkable, but the things inside them, few and ordinary as they were, caused me to pay attention to that low undercurrent of sensation once again. Those objects seemed somehow significant. They seemed to have something to say about the person who left them there. I pushed the distraction aside again. Upstairs we went through the bedrooms and the bathrooms. Again, we opened every hinged thing in the rooms and looked out at all the views. The remarkable thing about the views was that in every direction, and from each side of the house, there were a few parked cars, trees and fields, but no people. Later I would recall that, upon arriving, we drove into the development and up the driveway without seeing a single living soul. I wanted to live in a quiet spot and this one seemed, at least temporarily, completely deserted. Finally we came to a large bedroom, probably the master, and it was here that the sensation that I had pushed back twice pushed its way to the front of my awareness a third time, and with authority. The furnishings and accessories were neutral, they didn't say "woman's room," but that was the strong impression I received upon entering. I felt I was in the room of the lady of the house and I felt that it was impolite to be there, that we were intruding being in that room. Lastly, strangely, I received an impression about the room's owner. The thought came into my head that the lady whose room this was had passed. These fleeting feelings and odd suggestions were not usual for me, but although they were strange, they were without significance at the time so, again I refocused on the business of completing the tour and heading to the next, hopefully more desirable house on the list.

Tom suggested we see the basement before leaving, knowing a large basement was on my want list. We walked down from the second floor to the first and came to the basement door. The house was utterly quiet. It couldn't have been otherwise. We had just walked through every room in the building, had opened every closet, cabinet and drawer. We were in an empty house. Our views to the street revealed no traffic, no pedestrians, no activity of any kind. Tom held the door for us. My wife and I had just enough time to go down the short stairway and step onto the basement floor, before we heard five loud footsteps go across the floor above our heads. I suddenly felt terribly embarrassed finding myself casually walking around someone else's house with the owner at home. Tom, who was still stationed on the stairs, looked strange, but I took little notice of him in my haste to walk past him back upstairs to make my apologies. To get ourselves back onto the first floor took seconds, the split level design of the house made the stairway to the basement about half the length of an ordinary one. We shouted out as we walked to alert the homeowner that someone was in the house, but to our surprise, upon reaching the first-floor rooms, we could find no one. No one responded to our calls of hello. There had been no sound of a door opening or closing. The house was utterly quiet. Instinctively I went to the front door to see if perhaps we had heard the person leaving the house. I got outside and looked up and down the street. Finding no one there and no evidence of a car coming or going, I walked to the backyard. No one was there, or anywhere else in the area. Back inside we shrugged it off commenting on the strangeness of the person's unnaturally quick getaway. I briefly considered the possibility that someone could have been hiding behind the curtains and had then moved from one hiding place to another, but as soon as I thought it, I realized how ridiculous it was.

The rest of the day was spent rejecting other houses and finally, after a late lunch, we started the long trip back to our New York home. We discussed our prospects and went over the drawbacks of each place we had been to that time out. Hours had passed since the occurrence of the phantom footsteps. I hadn't thought about them after leaving the house until now. "What about those footsteps?" I asked my wife, finally taking time to analyze what had happened. No good answer ensued. The facts are these: if our intention had been to make sure we were alone in that house, we could not have made a more thorough inspection of the rooms and closets. Someone might have been around outside during the time we were there, but if they were, we did not see them, and there had definitely not been any sounds of a car, a door, or any other movement in the house until the footsteps sounded. In the time it took for us to hear the footsteps, react to them, and go back into the rooms upstairs, no one could have left the house, and if they had, we should have heard them continue to walk or at least have heard them use a door. No one was found in the house. No one was found outside it. The sound could not have been anything else but human footfall. There were five steps and they were hard, quick strides. The sound was of heeled shoes on a carpeted floor. Judging by our position in the basement, the footsteps seemed to start and end in the middle of the room above us. As we went over the stubborn facts of the event, it began to sink in to me that there would never be a good way to explain what had happened. For the first time in my life I had to consider the possibility of the impossible—that we might have been in a haunted house. One other thing bears mentioning: as I passed our agent Tom to go upstairs and explain our presence in the house to the person we assumed was walking around up there, I noticed that he wasn't looking very well and, also, that he had gone as white as a sheet.

I made the decision to not buy that house. I had no desire to see it again and took it for granted that I didn't have to. The sale of our New York home provided us with a healthy amount of money to work with in Pennsylvania's rural market and we could wait for the right place to come into view, even if it meant more four-hour Saturday morning drives. That was all right for us, but what about Tom? As an agent for the company showing that house, he would likely eventually have to go back. He would have to patiently do his walk through again for the next couple, and the next. Perhaps the time we were there together was not the first time Tom had had a problem with the house. Perhaps he was waiting in nervous anticipation for something to happen the whole time we were there. If he wasn't, he would be the next time.

It was this event that opened my eyes to the fact that there are some among us who are compelled to interact with strange places and their weird phenomena as part of the kind of work they do, or who are employed in ordinary trades housed in less than ordinary places.

What must it be like to have the keys to a haunted location and have to open that door again and again?

Tom knows.

Mercifully, I can only imagine.

2
Daily with the Dead

Revelations about haunted places are proliferating in this time of increased interest in the paranormal. Books, movies, and in recent years, a host of television series, have brought contact with the other side into a kind of morbid vogue. Young people seeking thrills go in search of "active" locations to experience something eerily exciting, or organize ghost hunts aimed at capturing recordings or images that they hope will validate the existence of those they believe are on the other side. Abandoned hospitals and factories, the shells of once grand houses, and historic battlefields are just a few of the settings enthusiasts find ripe for the hunt. In the private sector, the value of the designation of "haunted" has not escaped the attention of hoteliers, restaurateurs, and other businesses reliant on attracting the public, and some are willing to bank on the added attraction a resident ghost, real or engineered, will have on their establishment's power to draw. There is no doubt that the creepy allure ghost stories lend to a place can, to certain guests, elevate the attraction factor. Still, these patrons must consider that paranormal happenings, like winning lottery tickets, tend to happen randomly and be few and far between, but in either instance you have to be in it to win, so in they come. I can speak from some experience on this subject. My family and I have found ourselves in supposedly active locations for meals and as lodgers from time to time. It might be a result of this fad that we ended up spending time in such places in spite of the fact that we were not looking for them. I admit the hype can work and make an ordinary hour feel like a minor adventure, whether you believe anything has happened or not. I can further state that, on more than one occasion, a few mildly mysterious things have occurred that, thanks in a large part to the advertised reputation of our locale, made us feel that perhaps now we had our own personal stories to tell, even if it was just the wind. But here's the thing: it isn't always just the wind.

We diners, guests, and visitors have our evening of stories and glances up at the old portrait and up the old staircase between bites, have something to talk about on the ride home, and return to everyday life in the morning. Not so for some. Some people have to wait for the rest of us to clear out before they can start to end their day in their infamous workplace. Some have to turn off the lights on their way to the front door, feeling the blackness rushing up behind them, and having that last glance up the old staircase, the one in the dark! These are the people that know the real stories about the curious places we visit briefly, then leave behind. They are the ones among us that have to, whether they like it or not, turn that key every morning and step back inside. There are some who deal with an added layer of stress the rest of us can't ever imagine, because they believe they deal daily with the dead.

The following is a glimpse into one such person's acclimation to life in that uncomfortable flux known as a haunting.

In one of the myriad picturesque small towns that huddle between the fields that span central Pennsylvania, and which still carry a heavy inventory of pre-code, Victorian, and antebellum structures, sits a series of connected buildings that were, in the late 1800s, the property of a German immigrant who endeavored to build a business that would include a brewery, a tavern, and a hotel. He succeeded, and the distinctive establishment he brought into the world stands intact today and continues to serve guests in a manner that would surely make its founder proud. That is all well and good, but the old place has not survived without some change. The buildings are meticulously kept in as close to their original condition as possible, but since their erection, almost a century and a half ago, there have been additions of a sort. Some believe that the land, and the buildings that are built into it, like libations that ferment, have a character, and that that character changes with age. Some suggest that human emotions can leave an impression on a place, add a note so to speak, and direct the course of its nature as the original environment evolves to the present one. The present environment of the group of vintage buildings in question is, according to those who spend their days immersed in it, one that well represents the flavor of the present, while maintaining a strong, lingering aftertaste of the past.

Sara is a host employed at the brewery restaurant. She is also a young lady who had to make up her mind about sharing her space with "others" at an early age. She states, "I have had paranormal experiences since I was a child. I am open to these things . . . sensitive to them . . . I suppose I have accepted the fact that spirits do exist and are a part of life."

Before becoming an employee, she was first a patron and visited the establishment as a customer over the course of several years. According to Sara, many customers describe the ambiance at the old, dimly light buildings as "creepy" citing that uneasy feeling some places seem to exert on certain individuals and for which no specific source can be credited. Sara preferred to think of it as "mysterious." She told me, "There is a very noticeable vibe upon entering the building," and adds, "especially the first time you visit." But uncomfortable sensations are not all the hotel, dining hall, and brewery have to offer sensitive visitors. There are many and varied claims of strange activity throughout the complex of buildings that include objects being moved by unseen forces, an elegant apparition, and unseen presences that seem to be able to let which of the living they will or will not tolerate know exactly how they feel.

This certain selective intolerance has become a signature attribute of the hotel bar. It is of value to understand that in the days of its inception, the hotel bar area would have been almost exclusively for use by men. Although there were barmaids and the occasional female tavern owner, in many such places, before Prohibition necessitated the intermingling of men and women who found common refuge in speakeasies, a woman drinking unaccompanied by her husband would subject herself to being vilified, even to being labeled a harlot. Today, Sara describes that area of the hotel building as possessing a palpable, undeniably male character. She describes the sensation as being one similar to being in the presence of unfriendly company. She claims that she and other female employees sense that they are being psychically urged to leave when working that part of the hotel, and actually describe feeling intimidated by what they refer to as its "masculine energy." She says, "I do not feel welcome there. I feel like I am interrupting something, or trespassing every time I enter the room. It is not pleasant." In effect, female employees claim to feel the same unwelcoming pressure against their presence that ladies of the original era would have experienced should they have been rash enough to enter that domain of men. Claims of this sort are not uncommon, and not always psychical, but here the parallel makes an interesting argument in favor of the theory of, if not a haunting, perhaps the residual impression of human emotional activity.

But whether they find it pleasant or not, Sara and her sister employees must deal daily with the unwelcoming atmosphere that they find persists there. When I asked her to comment on her routine for making trips to the old bar room more positive, she replied that

she finds acknowledging any spirits that might be there of her impending entry works best for her. She will knock on the door before entering and announce herself out loud with a "Good afternoon" or "Hello." Says Sara, "Basically I talk to them. It makes me feel better about being in the space. If they are there, hopefully they appreciate the fact that I am trying to be respectful." If the old gentlemen are at all assuaged is not measurable. We can only report that their irritation persists, but does not escalate.

The bar might belong to the male entities, but womankind is represented at the hotel as well. One female form seen from time to time is a spirit Sara refers to as the site's "Lady in White." Harder to explain away than something you think you feel is the sight of a fellow human being right before your eyes, especially when they come and go from places without the usual access and egress required by corporeal beings, in short, an apparition. The "Lady in White," who gets her nickname due to the fact that she is seen wearing a long, light-colored dress in the style of an earlier time, seems aloof to the presence of the brewery's modern-day staff, be they female or male. In fact, one of the more common ways people experience her presence is by listening to her sing. Employees and customers alike have reported hearing a female voice singing in multiple areas of the buildings when no ladies are present, and when those that are deny being its source. This audible anomaly, which suggests that the "Lady" might be quite content with the modern incarnation of the business, continues to perplex guests, young and old. Recently, Sara was approached by a young boy who was dining with his family and who told her about hearing an unseen lady sing while he had his meal. The restaurant's baker, a woman who usually works alone and who does not play music while she works, has heard the voice, Sara reports, ". . . more times than she can count."

The "Lady" apparently makes her presence felt in other, less whimsical ways. Sara describes a narrow hallway leading to one of the kitchens that she and other employees have to use in the course of their duties. There, she experiences the feeling of being watched as she travels through. Sara says, "There is a female presence. . . Each time I walk down that hallway, I have this . . . feeling that, if I were to look into one of the rooms, she might be standing there." Coworkers agree, particularly a tour guide who recently had his first close encounter with the apparition after having worked there for years without incident. He claims to have seen the "Lady in White" in the hallway where others have reported they feel her standing close by. Sara recounted the incident for me. "He was carrying a dessert tray to the kitchen. He was struggling to put the tray in the fridge when he looked up and saw her standing there, in that narrow hallway I mentioned, staring at him. He was terrified . . ." Apparently the startled guide need not have been alarmed, for the lady held his gaze for only a moment before turning and walking noiselessly away.

How many hangers-on the buildings can boast no one knows, but the gentlemen at the bar and the musical "Lady" are surely not the entire population of extraordinary folks that tarry there. In paranormal circles, it is said that between the seen and the unseen there are persons of a shadowy variety. Observable but ill defined, these dark forms, or "shadow people" as they have come to be termed, are purported to move by quickly darting from place to place and are further supposed to be able to move through solid objects. Keep that in mind as you read Sara's account of a recent disturbing interruption to her daily routine.

"Two weeks ago, I was walking quickly through the kitchen into the dish room. As I entered the dish room, I saw someone out of the corner of my eye, standing near the wall. It was a shadowy figure. When I looked again, there was no one there. The dish room is small and if someone had been there, they would've had to cross my path to exit through the doorway. I immediately felt confused and a little creeped out. I tried to debunk the experience but there are no windows in the dish room, and no windows or light source that would point towards the room to cause a shadow. I have no explanation." The bartenders also claim to have seen shadowy things darting through the lobby when all the customers have left and they close the empty bar for the night. They also struggle to explain how some doors sometimes open and shut by themselves, and how glassware manages to fly off shelves when no one is anywhere near them.

The hotel bar, the narrow hallway, and the dish room are some of the places the timid among us, given the choice, might want to steer clear of. For visitors to Sara's place of work, those places might just be stops on a good natured ghost tour. To the people that call the old buildings home from morning to night, however, they are just that, parts of a home away from home, a haunted one, where an ordinary day can bump into an extraordinary encounter anytime and anywhere. Sara's earlier experiences have helped prepare her for life in an active location, but the sensations associated with always feeling that you are somehow moving through layers that don't exist in the outside world, coupled with the possible prospect of witnessing startling things around any corner, take their toll. Sara says, "When you work in a haunted place, you either allow yourself to be afraid . . . or you accept it. I have accepted that there are spirits at my job."

As in Sara's case, having had previous experiences can offer a degree of preparedness to those dealing with these kinds of situations in the workplace, but it is a rare person who can honestly state that the kind of phenomena reported to be going on at Sara's place of employment has ceased to impact them. Of ghosts in general Sara says, "...I dislike seeing them. I have seen a ghost before, and shadow people, too. Seeing them makes me feel uncomfortable. When you see a ghost, it's as though your brain just doesn't want to register it."

In spite of her dislike of apparitions, Sara is not afraid to live with the unusual happenings that plague her work day from time to time. For the people who find themselves in these uncomfortable situations and struggle, Sara recommends accepting that there is something there as a vital step toward managing their situation. As anyone can imagine, living with constant exposure to an environment that affects a person emotionally is, at best, a difficult and personal thing. Sara's little ceremonies of knocking before entering a room, or talking out loud create a sense of partial control. These practices can help keep a lid on a person's sense of panic. Fellow employees can offer support, but usually only if they are similarly affected, and then only if they are the kind willing to be open about something as stigmatized as the possible existence of paranormal activity.

To some hearing complaints like these, a change of career comes to mind as a quick fix for someone stuck in a situation that so upsets them. Some can and do, but try taking that advice seriously yourself for a moment, and a whole host of reasons why that might not always be so easy will quickly present itself. As for the population at large, they will more than likely be unsympathetic to anyone claiming to be suffering from paranormal fatigue. On that divide, Sara says, "As for people who do not believe, well, I think they won't allow themselves to believe. It's hard for me to relate to someone who has never had a paranormal experience, because I've had countless experiences and I know what I have seen, heard, and felt."

Weeks after my initial interview with Sara, I visited her at the location to go over her story for a final time. We sat at a table not far from the bar with the misogynistic reputation. Before I left her, she let me know that the previous evening something else strange had occurred. She told me she was sitting at the same table we were currently occupying while watching a male coworker pick up small glasses lined up on the wide, sturdy counter for collection. The young man was taking them one by one from the bar and setting them on to a tray he held with his other hand. Suddenly, without evidence of the application of any external force, one of the glasses left the counter, traveled about six feet through the air, and shattered on the stone floor. The glass was quickly swept up, and the bartender, with equal quickness, rushed to apply logic to the situation saying, "The counter isn't level on that part." It is odd how some people will readily suggest something clearly absurd in an attempt to "take the curse off" an uncomfortable situation. The bar counter I observed was not perceptibly uneven, and definitely not uneven enough to cause an empty glass to take flight the way the one observed the previous evening had. Any counter that *was* would be a constant potential hazard in a place that serves drinks on it day and night. Denial is another way individuals deal with the presence of unexplainable phenomena occurring in places they have no choice but to remain in. Sara swears that she observed the glass go unaided from stationary to mobile and fly to the ground. Having never seen anything like that myself I commented, "That's amazing." Sara shrugged, and smiled as if to say, "Welcome to my world."

In the future, a body of recognized scientific works might validate the accounts of people like Sara and the vast number of others like her. Until then, healthy human skepticism fills in the blanks in paranormal logic with equally theoretical, but more earthly explanations, closes the case, and moves along.

For now, to those like her who carry the keys to these, as yet, unsolved places, Sara shares this advice, "Do not be afraid, but do not doubt what you are experiencing. You're not going crazy, you're not in danger, just be confident, and trust what your senses are telling you."

Those words could serve as a mantra for those who believe they are sharing quarters with others from another time and in an altered state, for those who might be dealing daily with the dead.

Some people don't like to be alone in empty houses, especially strange ones. Consider the plight of the real estate agent for whom empty or abandoned homes represent the landscape of their every day. Lonely though they might seem at times, the average home for sale is deliberately staged, or swept and tidy if empty, to create as positive an impression as possible. The vast majority of homes that change hands do so because something about them appealed to the new owner, placing it above all others being considered. It might take time, but eventually almost all will have their buyer.

Almost all, but not all.

In the real estate field there is a term for places that have a particular taint that makes them unattractive, and that no amount of decorating or scrubbing can expunge. That term is "stigmatized" and it is used to label properties that have either been the scenes of crimes, or of deaths resulting from suicide or murder, and not least of all, of paranormal events. Defamed or not, once a property is on the market it becomes someone's mission to move it.

The following narrative centers on the true account of a real estate agent, we'll call him Ron, whose discomfort was brought about not because of his time spent in empty houses, but because he spent time in one that was not.

3
Worse Than Empty

Always eager to take on a good property, Ron arrived well equipped and considerably early to preview a home newly available to him in one of his favorite parts of his territory, the North Oakland neighborhood of Pittsburgh, Pennsylvania. The area was a personal favorite of his for two reasons. The first was the fact that Ron had grown up in the area and, like most people, had a definite fondness for his old home town. Spending time back on familiar streets was a nostalgic perk. He hadn't lived there for some years at the time of the events that were to follow, but years could not dull the feeling of comfort brought about by the sight of old, familiar places, and the knowledge that, at least occasionally, they were still a part of his life. Years ago, it was on these streets that he would pass entire summer vacations playing ball games and meeting friends. His first job and his first big sale all happened within the boundaries of this old East Allegheny neighborhood. The second attraction Oakland held for Ron was the fact that, for one reason or another, he had always done well there as far as quick sales were concerned. It was his "Kill Zone" as he liked to refer to it. Both these private pleasures, which had gladdened, and provided Ron with such confidence, and for so long, would soon be challenged. Soon neither would be enough to make Ron return to one particular house in North Oakland ever again.

It was a warm, sunny Friday morning when Ron pulled into the driveway of the impressive, old two-story brick and half-timbered building on Bayard Street with the Landry Real Estate sign on the front lawn. He halted his car in front of heavy wooden garage doors that hung on immense iron hinges, a detail indicative of 1920s construction. If Ron was any judge of turn of the century, "old money" homes, and he was, there would be 4,500 square feet-plus of thick plaster walls and dark, polished wood trim inside. His was the only car on the driveway. Two porthole shaped windows set in the garage doors allowed Ron to gauge if anyone else was likely to be present at the house today. Ron walked up to one of the windows, shielded his eyes from the glare and looked in. He was pleased to see that the space was empty. No vehicle in either the driveway or garage usually meant nobody home. The opportunity for privacy was a boon. It meant Ron could take his time and really drink in the home's features as well as do some amateur home inspection on the side. Ron liked what he had seen so far, made note of the dimensions and condition of the driveway, and went around to the portico covered front entrance, in happy anticipation of yet another healthy North Oakland commission.

Ron used his key to open the lock box, retrieved the front door key, and undid the deadbolt. Its snap echoed loudly inside. As he stepped into the front room, Ron shouted an automatic "Hello." His greeting resounded inside the void of the empty first floor, and decayed with a hollow ring. He paused for a moment to listen and make sure there was no one coming in response to his call, then, satisfied that he was alone, he shut the door behind him. Inside, the

ceilings were high and the rooms large. Their size helped to create a profound sense of emptiness. The view from where he stood in the foyer revealed, in the distance, the back door leading out to a garden. To the left was the staircase to the second floor landing, wide, with a heavy squared newel post, its oak surfaces sporting the expected dark umber patina of age. Wainscoting panels graced the lower third of the walls throughout the ground floor. The runner left on the stairs was of quality, probably Axminster Ron guessed, but downstairs the hardwood floors were bare, and only covered here and there with scraps of a dull pink builder's paper laid there by workmen and crisscrossed with dusty footprints.

Evidently work was being done to the house. Power tools, cables, even a work radio were in different places around the floors. A cup of coffee, now cold and with a thin floating layer of dust across its surface, was perched on a knee wall between the hallway and the large parlor. Ron could see no evidence of recent activity. Apparently, the contractors had brought their equipment in, but not started their work.

As with most agents, kitchens and bathrooms were always first on Ron's checklist. Walking through a spacious drawing room, and noting the floor to ceiling built-ins and fireplace as he went, Ron came to the kitchen. He surveyed it with approval. An updated kitchen, as this one was, and one so large, is a most valuable selling point. Ron would use his phone's camera to photograph the room. He raised the shade on one of the kitchen windows for light, but before he could frame the first shot, Ron stopped to hone in on what appeared to be a faint interior sound. Walls in houses from this period of construction are always solid and wide. They afford a vacuum-like silence for those inside. This silence was now being broken by what sounded like movement coming from somewhere upstairs. The sound was of a dull thudding, as if some heavy object were being walked across a carpeted floor. Ron took a few steps back into the adjacent room. He stopped, and listened again. A few seconds of silence and then the bumping sound resumed. "Hello?"

he called loud enough, he thought, to reach the people upstairs. He paused anticipating acknowledgment. When none came, he walked back to the front room and looked up toward the top of the stairs. Then, not in response, but sounding as if it was oblivious to Ron's presence, a voice floated down from the upper story of the house. It was a man's voice, deep and strangely distant sounding for someone just one floor above. What the man was saying, Ron could not tell. His words sounded garbled or slurred, or he might have been speaking in a foreign language. Although the words were indistinct, the tone was easy to interpret. This was the sound of someone in an ill humor. Ron stood still and listened, straining to catch any word. Eventually the thumping sound stopped, but the voice continued, increasing slightly in volume. Although the voice Ron was hearing had pitch and tone, and was forming words, something about it was different. Some quality seemed to be either added or missing. Something indefinable was wrong. It put him on guard enough to keep him from calling out again. Ron remained mostly curious about the voice until its cadence evolved into what sounded like grunts, or short shouts. At that change, Ron felt a queasiness sprout in the pit of his stomach. The threatening quality of the muted words alarmed him. He felt that the aggression in the voice was, for some reason, aimed specifically at him. It was illogical, but Ron decided to heed his instinct to remove himself with haste. Turning away from the staircase, Ron went back out through the front door as quietly as he could, shut it, bolted it, and refastened the lock box device. Standing outside Ron listened intently for any sign of the voice or any evidence that someone inside was coming downstairs to investigate. Although he did not want to confront the angry author of the tirade, he waited a full half-a-minute listening at the door, believing the man would have heard the bolt snap and come down to see who was there. For the duration of that time, however, he did not hear any further sounds. The house was completely silent again.

In a disturbed state, and certain that he would not be going back into the house again that day, Ron walked back to his car. He turned over the engine, and started backing slowly down the driveway. As the vehicle rolled halfway to the street, the dormer windows of the attic came into view and caught his eye. Ron gently stopped the car in order to maintain his view of them. They were vacant, reflecting only the bright, intense sky, with white sheer curtains hanging loosely behind them. Next, an unbidden bizarre notion entered Ron's mind. He began to entertain the idea that if he continued to stare up at the windows, he might cause the curtains to sweep aside, that his continued gaze would somehow provoke them to violently part and reveal someone or something standing behind. Ron idled there briefly, then, as if coming to, forced his stare away from the house, re-focused on his rear-view mirror, and finished entering the roadway. He did not look back as he pulled away.

As he drove, Ron went over the events at the house. With time to think, Ron wondered if that voice didn't belong to one of the workers whose equipment he saw scattered downstairs. Workmen often curse their tools when a job isn't going smoothly. There was no reason why the anger in the voice Ron heard should have been directed toward him. The speaker never acknowledged his calls of hello, and gave the impression that he was unaware that anyone else was in the house. Why then, did Ron react the way he did? He wasn't ordinarily the type to be intimidated. As Ron continued, he felt out of sorts and did not look left or right, as was his custom, to catch glances of beloved landmarks around his old home town. It was as if the episode at the house had affected him on some emotional level. In this uncharacteristic manner, he drove the several miles back to his office in silence, unsuccessfully trying to make sense of what he had just experienced.

Back at the office, where no one had expected Ron to view the house on Bayard Street, he was asked no questions, and he volunteered no details about his brief visit or the premature exit he felt forced to make. As the day progressed, a series of plausible scenarios for everything that happened that morning presented themselves to Ron, providing him with a lifeline back to normalcy. In between, business kept his mind otherwise occupied, so by the time he was home again, Ron was completely over his concerns about what might have, or might not have, happened to him that morning. That night the only thing on his mind as he prepared to retire, was that tomorrow was Saturday, and he could afford to sleep off his questions, his confusion, and the whole unpleasant episode. Later, lying in bed, Ron's thoughts returned for a last time to the details of the morning's events. He went over all the explanations he had come up with since, and was pleased at how they fit together to put the mystery to rest. It was only then, when he was so close to a sense of resolution, that Ron recalled that to enter the house he had had to use the lock box key taken from the office. In order for anyone to gain similar access they would need that same key as every door to the vacant house on Bayard was now locked from the outside.

A week later Ron had a client who was looking for an impressive older home in town for she and her husband. She would be editing the field alone until her spouse could get away and add his opinion to the houses left standing. Ron reviewed properties in the North Oakland area and realized the place on Bayard represented a good fit. He was overdue for a return, and his first official showing would double as his own first comprehensive look at the property. The incident with what he now believed was merely a gruff worker, and the unusual feelings Ron had, were rendered less worrisome by the time that had elapsed, and he had no trepidations about going back. Any workmen would have completed their tasks by now, or, he hoped, be having a better day.

When they rolled up onto the driveway, Ron's client, a Mrs. Fulton, was instantly pleased by the outer features of the house and approved of its location, only a few blocks away from the center of town. Ron was enjoying this early positive response as he once again removed the front door key and let his guest precede him into the spacious front room. The woman was immediately drawn to the fine runner on the stairs, and took little notice of the pieces of construction equipment that were the only things present in the otherwise empty rooms. They presented an ordinary scene to a house hunter getting used to touring older homes for sale, but to Ron there was something slightly sinister about the display of scattered gear. Ron realized that these were the selfsame tools he had seen a week earlier and he was sure that they were all in exactly the same positions he had last seen them in. Some of the liquid in the coffee cup had evaporated, and the dust layer on it and everything else, was increased by an even amount. They no longer represented everyday items temporarily set aside for break time. The workmen had not returned for at least the week since he had first been there. To Ron, the tools now looked less like they were temporarily out of action and more like they had been abandoned.

The hair raised slightly on Ron's arms as he contemplated the tableau of discarded items. Had the crew heard or seen anything that could have made them leave the house in haste? Had something frightened them to such a degree that they refused to return, even to reclaim these valuable tools of their trade? He could not help creating a scene in his mind of the crew pausing in their work to listen to a disturbance coming from somewhere on the second floor.

Ron was roused from his musings by his client's voice as she emerged from the kitchen, where she had moved on to without him, asking him something about the previous owner.

"I'm sorry?" he said prompting her to re-ask her question.

"Is the owner at home?" she asked. "I hear someone upstairs and if it's all right, I'd like to ask them something about the gas appliances."

The churn in his gut he had felt the first day was starting again as he stood still in an attempt to detect any noise that, as Mrs. Fulton had stated, might be emanating from the second floor. His wait was short. Ron and his client made eye contact, he nervously, she pointing at the ceiling and smiling, acknowledging the distinct noises of things being moved across a carpeted floor somewhere above them.

"Do you think we could speak to them? I'd like to know about

the neighborhood as well," asked Ron's buyer, her eyes searching his for encouragement.

With effort, Ron tried to dissuade her. "I think those must be workmen," he managed. "The owners moved out of state. I can help you with any questions." He addressed her, but his attention was now completely invested in listening to the sounds upstairs.

"Thanks," the woman replied heading back to the kitchen. "It's just that I know nothing about gas ovens or stoves, although I know cooking with a live flame is supposed to be the best way. Oh," she added turning, "what kind of work *are* they doing to the house?"

Ron listened again to the thuds coming from above and wondered that himself. "I'm not sure," he admitted.

"I'd like to see," she said. "I didn't know there were repairs being made."

She came alongside indicating a desire that they go upstairs together. Ron had been fighting to keep a feeling of panic at bay. Having a client present forced him to do what was expected of him professionally, but he struggled with a sense of dread that increased the closer they got to the stairs. "Hello!" Ron called up. No one called back, but a voice began to emerge from within the muddy hodgepodge of the noise. The voice they heard was strange to one, familiar to the other. Ron instantly recognized the voice as that of the man whose threatening manner had caused him to retreat the last time.

The voice was low with the same angry tone, as if taking up where Ron had left it all those days ago. The two began to climb the stairs when there was a louder thud. That made them pause. Ron turned to the woman who was a step behind him. She looked up at Ron, now with a hint of budding apprehension in her eyes. "Hello! We're viewing the house! Landry Realty!" Ron shouted. The person behind the voice continued to ignore Ron's calls, but as they ascended the stairs the noises seemed to recede. That helped Ron feel better about continuing up. Ron and his client stood still when they reached the landing. Ron called a final "Hello?" There was now not only no

reply, but the sounds of movement and the man's voice had been replaced by a heavy, total silence.

An open bedroom door was directly opposite them. Ron walked cautiously forward and looked inside. The room was utterly vacant. Without another word and keeping close together, the two looked into the second and third bedrooms confirming that they, too, were empty. Ron noticed that as they walked, each step they took on the hard wooden floors was audible, even loud in contrast to the silence of the empty hall. It was not lost on either of them that no such sound accompanied the person's voice as it had retreated to wherever on that floor that someone now was. They then looked into the last room on the floor, the bathroom at the end of the hall. Pushing the door aside revealed that it was as unoccupied as the others. Where and why was this person hiding, Ron wondered, and what would be in store when they found him?

The only place left was the room with the dormer windows Ron had inexplicably fixated on from the driveway that first day. Ron softly approached the door, Mrs. Fulton, uninterested in going further, remained tied to her spot in the hallway. Settling in front of the door, Ron listened for any indication of movement from the other side. His neck and shoulders tingled as he uttered a final questioning, "Hello?" He put his hand on the doorknob and tried it to see if the door was locked. When it gave all the way, he held the door closed for a moment then pushed it into the room. It scraped the floor as Ron swung it all the way in. He was steeled for an encounter he knew would be uncomfortable, even weird, but he was completely unprepared for what he discovered then. He struggled to comprehend how this, the last possible place in the house for anyone to be, could be as empty as all the previous rooms were.

Ron's client had turned and started walking back to the staircase without waiting for him. He wanted to apologize or make some excuse, but there was no good excuse or explanation for what was happening. Her heels clunked loudly, quickly down the stairs ahead of him to a tempo that indicated both urgency and fear. When he reached the first floor, Mrs. Fulton was already outside and continuing in the direction of the car. Having to consider the wellbeing of Ron's client allowed his mind to temporarily occupy itself in familiar, normal territory. That helped him to refrain from thinking too much about the noises and the voice they had both just heard coming from the emptiest of empty houses. As before, he shut the door and re-latched the bolt keeping his ears alert for the sound of pursuing footsteps or an angry word. Through a background of confused emotions, Ron imagined he felt another's eyes observing him, strongly willing him to leave from somewhere, perhaps the attic window, perhaps right on the other side of the very door he was busy locking. Inwardly he assured the originator of that sentiment not to worry, that the message had been well received. Ron, at least, would not intrude again.

Ron drove his client back to the office where her own car was parked. He could not tell if the woman was angry, frightened, or in the same kind of daze he found himself in after his first encounter with the house. In any case, the effect was the same, neither spoke a word the entire drive back.

After delivering his client to her car, Ron finally found voice enough to eke out a confused apology. She drove off, still without a word to Ron, after which he went into the office and sat, head in hands, at his desk. After a long pause in which he mulled over the situation, Ron got up and strode out of his office, anger starting to replace the unease his experience had caused him. This anger would find its target in the person of Ron's boss, the no-nonsense senior manager who had asked Ron to move the property. Entering his supervisor's office and boiling over he said, "I'm not going back in that house again! Got it? I'm done! I've had it with that damn place!" Before he could receive feedback, Ron turned and left the building. He did not return for the rest of the day.

To his surprise, Ron was met with curt, but affable tolerance the next day. His boss said good morning and stayed out of his way. Ron had spent hours going over what he would say in answer to questions about the house and his behavior, but those questions never came. Ron thought it was strange that he was never reprimanded for his outburst and blunt refusal to complete a sale. Agents are usually only excused from that if the office knows of some problem with a property that is so serious it renders it unsellable. The reason for the pass he had been given came to Ron in drips. Apparently the property had a reputation among Ron's peers for having a "creepy atmosphere." He discovered that there were two camps among them, those who scoffed at the idea and used it as fodder for jokes, and those that had been there.

There is no doubt that avoidance is a strategy that works when seeking solutions to returning to uninviting locations, but it is an option that depends on circumstances often out of the individual's control. If required to show the property again, the real "Ron" would have had to find some other way to handle his anxiety and cope with the audio phenomena that appeared to be the signature of the disgruntled, spectral lodger of the vacant house. As a professional, "Ron" is obliged to refrain from misrepresenting or concealing facts about a property. Even if he had found a way of normalizing the experience, it would have been a challenge to convince interested parties that the reduced price and desirable location more than made up for the house's intermittent, mind-bending peculiarity.

The subject of our story is still doing quite well connecting buyers with quality homes in North Oakland. The area continues to be a combination Memory Lane and Kill Zone for him, full of echoes of the past and hope for the future. The only difference now is that it also reminds him of a certain two-story brick and half-timbered building on Bayard Street that he had to decline the trade of, and that despite having all the right appointments, and sitting on a prime piece of property, is still for sale, and still, people claim, quite empty.

4
Finders Weepers

Being the proprietors of a bed and breakfast is a demanding occupation on many fronts. Paramount is that the customer be satisfied. Catering to the expectations of numerous and varied types is an art akin to improvisation. Accounting, marketing, maintenance, and mechanical breakdowns are all part of any host's season. Langdon and Beth Moore have been, are, and plan on continuing to be, up to these daunting tasks until the day they decide to retire. Indeed, after decades in the business, there isn't much that can really worry them as innkeepers, except for one solid exception. Any time a guest reports something has gone missing—a book, or a comb, or the smallest, least valuable thing—the Moores go on the alert, and brace themselves for a situation no amount of experience has so far been able to ease.

In the 1970s, on New York's Long Island, Langdon and Beth Moore made average livings working average jobs. The predictable result was an average life that neither found distasteful, but that neither cared to settle for in perpetuity. The joy of their lives at the time of this introduction was their daughter, Linda, age two. On weekends, the family's favorite escape from the doldrums was to drive out to the East End, the villages and hamlets of the island's North Fork peninsula, for the kind of peace and quiet that was a treasured balm after a work week in the crowded, traffic filled suburbs of New York City.

In those days, on the North Fork, potato farms, apple orchards, and roadside stands, created a homey environment the two never tired of. Vineyards, which were just starting to dot the area, and views of the Long Island Sound, the body of water north of the land mass, completed a picture of a simpler, elegant life. Langdon and Beth usually drove to and from their favorite spot in the same day, but, once they decided to extend their pleasure, and be guests at a bed and breakfast establishment near the ocean. They had arranged to stay at a restored farmhouse friends had visited earlier and recommended highly. "No children or dogs please" meant Linda would stay with Beth's mother for the weekend.

Langdon and Beth pulled into the driveway of their temporary lodgings on a perfect summer morning. From the sun bleached shingles that clad the exterior to the gracious antiques within, the old house was magnificent in the eyes of the young couple. When it came to a list of the highlights of their visit, this time the seductive comfort and calm of the guest house trumped all the regular attractions the area had to offer. For the Moores the experience was liberating and transformative.

Driving home, after tarrying as long as possible on the second day, the couple began reciting all the things they liked best about the inn. Even after picking up Linda, their reminiscing continued into the night, and slowly a theme crept into their conversation. What, they wondered, would each not give to change places with their Farmhouse host? They played with the idea of abandoning everything and starting anew as owners of their own bed and breakfast out east. It was a dream they could not act upon then, but by and by it became a serious goal. They planned in the hopes that an opportunity would one day present itself and even started to talk to Linda in terms of "when we move to the farmhouse."

By the mid-1970s, a struggle for Long Island farmers produced the opportunity the Moores had kept their feelers out for. Smaller potato farms found themselves competing with larger western concerns for their market share. Some retooled and joined ranks of the early vineyards. Others parceled out their acreage to developers or anyone who was interested in buying the land. Motivated by the new availability of lots, the couple reserved every weekend for the express purpose of finding the future sight of Langdon House, or Beth's Nest, or whatever the favored nickname was that week.

Then, finally, the Moores, all three of them, drove out to see the house that would eventually become their home, business, and legacy. As if tailor made for the couple's intended use, the old farmhouse they toured offered five bedrooms. The fine, rustic home was built in 1792, an exciting statistic as far as the Moores were concerned, and although in need of much renovation, an undeniable diamond in the rough. There was a fireplace in almost every room, and exposed beam ceilings crowned the kitchen and dining rooms. With its two acres of land, the Moores could not have designed a more perfect plot. When they learned that the condition of the house brought it within the lower end of their price range, Langdon and Beth claimed the house on the spot. They thanked their agent, thanked providence, celebrated with a superb meal, and wondered what they were going to do. As of that moment they had two mortgages and only a vague idea of what the word "renovations" would translate to in dollars.

Langdon and Beth had help, but worked on restoring their future residence themselves as much as possible to reduce cost, and because they loved being part of the piecemeal manifestation of their dream. There was no shortage of unexpected costs as they reconditioned the building from the basement up. As it turned out, though, there was one particularly unexpected component to doing so.

Admittedly, the building was often in a state of disarray during that year the Moores labored away, but often, and in the strangest way, things would suddenly go missing. This series of disappearances started with small hand tools. Mr. Moore, or one of the contractors, would be using a pair of pliers or a screwdriver, remember putting it down in the area where they were working, and then, when they wanted it again, be unable to find it, either where it should have been, or anywhere. Naturally, they believed that these things must have either rolled away or been kicked, ending up under something

else on the site or into a gap somewhere. There was no alternate explanation, so they dealt with the nuisance by finding replacements and refocusing on their work. As days progressed, however, other, less easily misplaced items started suffering the same fate. Langdon recalls a piece of Beth's jewelry, a thin chain bracelet, she had taken off and left on a window ledge. It wasn't valuable enough to be the target of a thief, but theft would have been hard to prove in any case because when the piece was lost, Beth was the only person on the property. She searched the room thoroughly to no avail. She never heard a sound to indicate the object fell, was picked up, or that any person or animal came into or went out of the room. It seemed to have simply evaporated. Another odd item to have rolled away or been swept aside was a can of beer Langdon was sipping from on a hot day as he was alone in the house sanding floors. Generally, when someone puts down their beverage, they look where they are setting it so they won't place it where it could be knocked over and spilled. Langdon set his can down on a stack of wood beside him on the floor. A short time later, he left the room to get more discs for the sanding machine. After returning, he continued working, but the next time he paused for a drink the can was gone. There was no spill on the floor to indicate that it had fallen. Also, his work had coated the entire floor with dust resulting from the grinding of the wood planks. His footprints were obvious on the delicate coating. He saw his own trail from the room out and back in again, but observed no other marks on the floor. He searched for the missing item, but knew it was not, could not, be anywhere else in the room.

Langdon stepped outside and scanned the area for movement. He listened for anything that might indicate that he wasn't completely alone. The silence he usually treasured, this time, was unwelcome. Even the gulls and crows were distant sounding, seeming to prefer neighboring lots rather than Langdon's, and the far away quality of their calls compounded the feeling of desolation. Frustrated, Langdon settled on the only explanation he could. He blamed himself for forgetting what he had done with the missing can, putting it down

to fatigue and the stress of the renovation and it's rapidly mounting price tag. This was his choice only because he had no other, but even as he made up his mind to resign to it, serious doubt destroyed any comfort it might have given him. What happened next would take him even further out into a sea of doubt and confoundment.

The day after the beer can mysteriously took its leave, Langdon returned to the house to continue work on the floors. Other workers were scheduled to be there, and as he pulled up to the house, he saw a panel van parked in the driveway. Everyone knew where the spare key was hidden, and as he exited his car, Langdon could hear men, having let themselves in, going about their business. Langdon climbed the stairs to the front porch, but before he could reach for the door, something caught his eye. Resting precariously on the narrow hand rail was a pair of pliers. He immediately recognized them as a pair he had lost days before when ripping molding away from the base boards. Something about the manner in which they were left, almost as if displayed there, seemed odd to Langdon. He was anxious to hear where they had finally been found. He took them into the house and went upstairs to let the others inside know he had arrived. After pleasantries, Langdon asked if any of them had found the pliers and left them on the porch rail for him. The men replied that they had not, then asked Langdon if it had been he who had found their missing tape measure and left that item on their ladder. When Langdon confessed he knew nothing about it, the men shrugged and assumed someone else working at the house had done them the favor. Langdon knew no one else besides himself had been in the house for days since those men had last been there, but saw no value in sharing that aside. Langdon worked distractedly all day. Paramount on his mind was sorting out how the disappearances and reappearances of these objects was being done. Someone, he reasoned, had to be coming into the house at night to play pranks. He felt uneasy with the idea of a trespasser disrespecting the property where he was shortly to bring his wife and young daughter. When the others left that day, Langdon explained that, with his and other people's property scattered around the vacant house, he thought it would be best to keep the house locked and hold on to the spare key from now on. He would open the house when someone needed access, and ask everyone to be sure to turn the doorknob switch to the locked position before shutting it behind them. That seemed to put an end to the mischief for the remaining weeks that passed before the house was ready to receive the family. On the day the Moores moved in, Beth and Linda arrived at the house a few hours before the truck with their belongings was to arrive, to open the house and generally get things ready. Beth decided to sweep all the floors one more time to get as much of the construction dust off them as possible before the furniture and carpets were put in place. She was sweeping out the corner of one of the bedrooms when, to her amazement, her missing bracelet was pushed into the center of the floor by the broom. How it had gotten there she had no idea, but she was happy to have it back and considered its return a good omen for their future life in the old farmhouse.

Later, she would revise that interpretation.

Besides repairing and decorating the house during the months leading up to moving day, Langdon and Beth had also been busy finalizing their business plan. Langdon continued to work at his job while they broke into the hospitality industry one couple or small family at a time. Beth loved having guests and providing them with her version of the restful paradise she and Langdon had experienced years ago when they played the role of visitors. The first year was a slow process of learning how to attract business when there wasn't any and how to manage it when there was. Because of their dedication to their guests, and because the house, in its new incarnation, was truly inviting, word of mouth business slowly but steadily rewarded the Moores. During this time of growth, the curious tendency for small objects to vanish from where the family, and now guests, had recently left them was still an occasional concern.

The busier days and the frequent comings and goings of groups made it easier to rationalize the sporadic losses. Still, it was not uncommon for the Moores, when saying their goodbyes to guests, to add a promise to forward lost items as soon as they were found.

In their second year in business, the Moores received another young family as guests who would become regular visitors as well as friends. The Connellys hailed from a town called Franklin Square, on the western half of the island, and brought with them their daughter Sadie who was six, the same age as Linda. Like their parents, the two young girls got along like old friends right away. Sadie wore glasses to read, but was like her new playmate in every other respect. The two were allowed to be away for hours exploring the property before Langdon and Mr. Connelly went out to fetch them back for lunch. The next day, the Connelly's asked Beth if Linda could accompany them on a trip to the beach. After that, the girls were inseparable until Sunday morning came and Sadie and her parents had to start the long drive back home. As the family were saying goodbyes and taking their places in the car, Mrs. Connelly noticed that Sadie did not have her glasses. Sadie looked in her bag, but did not find them. She and Linda ran up to the room the Connellys had occupied and made a thorough search for the missing item. After looking into, and under, everything in the room, the girls returned empty handed. Sadie was sure she had not taken them to the beach so it was assumed the glasses were somewhere in the house. Because it was getting late, and as a spare pair waited at home, the Moores once again exchanged goodbyes with their guests while promising to forward the errant object just as soon as it was found. After a search of the rooms, it was determined that Sadie must have dropped her glasses somewhere outside when the girls were exploring the first day, and the case was closed.

A year passed and business at the historic Driftwood Inn, as it had finally been christened, increased again. In the time that passed since the Connelly's first visit, Linda and Sadie kept in touch through letters, and it was through one of these that the Moores learned that Sadie and her parents intended to reserve another weekend at their home. It was the middle of July when the Moores prepared to receive their guests once again. The same room had been reserved for them as before and Linda camped by the street facing window of her room to wait for Sadie's car to appear on the horizon. Eventually Langdon and Beth heard Linda's excited cries of "They're here!" carry down to them from upstairs. The two rose to go to the porch from where they would receive their guests. As they walked from the parlor to the hallway, however, they froze in their steps as if they had both just been confronted by a blast of chilling air. Beth gasped, then held her breath. She began to tremble. Langdon's mind raced as he tried to reason how Sadie's glasses could possibly be lying dead center on the hallway floor, temples spread apart and facing them. Seconds later, the sound of Linda coming down the stairs pressed Langdon to rush forward and remove the object. An inner sense communicated to him that his daughter should not see the weird display. When the little girl stood at the door next to Langdon, she stared at him in such a way that he knew he must have looked shaken.

He forced a smile and said, "Why don't you go outside and see your friend honey."

Linda said, "Okay." Then she added, "Why is Mommy crying?"

Langdon turned to see Beth holding both hands to her mouth, tears visible on her cheeks. Langdon turned back to his daughter and said, "Mommy feels sick, honey. She'll be all right. It's okay. Just go and tell Sadie's parents to come in and we'll be right down."

Linda smiled and went out to the porch to greet her guests.

Langdon took Beth back upstairs to their room where they had a brief discussion about what had just happened and how they were going to handle it. Sadie's glasses had been gone for a year. The materialization of this object was not open to discussion in the quasi-comfortable terms of absent mindedness, nest building animals, or a stealthy, unseen, unknown neighbor's child. The timing of the reappearance, on the day of Sadie's return, only minutes before she would walk through the door, and in an area the family had walked through all morning was a statement, the interpretation of which was, "I am real. I am here. Now you believe."

Beth pleaded for a few minutes to recover before facing her guests. She confessed that she had long felt uneasy about the disappearing items, and that she had experienced things being suddenly gone from where she had left them only to reappear in different parts of the house hours later, many times when Langdon was away. Whenever she asked Linda if she had taken the objects, the child always denied it, and Beth saw nothing in her behavior to make her doubt her daughter's word. When things started disappearing when Linda was at school, Beth even began to question her sanity, but Linda also complained of losing things that would later turn up in places she had not recently been. Until now, she refused to allow herself to think in any other terms for fear of becoming uncomfortable in her own home, but today's occurrence left Beth no choice but to concede that there was something unnatural about the old farmhouse. Langdon revealed that he had been keeping to himself the fact that he had also been missing things, and that ever since his experience with the vanishing beer can, he suspected that something was not quite right about the place and about the way people kept losing things on their property.

The incident with Sadie's glasses was a shock, but speaking honestly about the situation at their home offered some much needed relief. A short time later, when the Moores came down to welcome their guests, they made apologies for Beth's not feeling well, and returned Sadie's glasses, saying that they had found them outside some time ago but had forgotten about them until today. They had a quiet, friendly visit with their company, but spent almost every minute of it anxious should Sadie's glasses go missing again. The following Sunday evening Sadie and her parents prepared to leave, going over a verbal checklist to make sure they did not leave anything behind. Sadie was asked to produce both pairs of glasses, which she did, to cheers, and then the family waved a final farewell and drove off toward home.

That night, Langdon and Beth struggled with the new reality of their situation. The house was everything to them, their home, their business, and, they hoped, something they would leave to Linda and *her* family someday. They now had to ask themselves if they were strong enough to live with something they could not understand or control, to tolerate things in their own home that made tenuous their very sense of normalcy. Now, when they turned the key in the front door and entered, it would be to a house that only looked empty, to a peace and quiet that was granted rather than invariable. Initially, Beth felt she could not live with the haunting, asking Langdon to consider leaving. He was less inclined to give up everything they had built and asked Beth to be patient and weigh her decision. It was some time before either Beth or Langdon felt any level of comfort again, but like anyone wishing to protect the things dear to them, they found ways to adapt, even to the fact of their ghostly borrower. To shield her, the situation was never discussed with Linda.

One unexpected aftereffect of the day the glasses appeared on the hallway floor, was that whoever, or whatever, was responsible for the vanishing objects seemed to have gained some measure of appeasement from either the act, or from the change in the Moores it forced them to make. Incidents of missing objects became fewer and farther between. Throughout the years guests would occasionally ask their hosts if they had happened to see some small missing item. At such times, the Moores would involuntarily pause, recompose, and then assure their guests that they would definitely forward the missing article, just as soon as it turned up.

A die-hard skeptic, the gentleman who is the real "Langdon" and who really found the pair of glasses waiting for him in the middle of the floor after a one year hiatus told me, "I must tell you I am not a believer of weird phenomena. My natural inclination would be to debunk any such tale," but adds, "Needless to say, we had walked through the area thousands of times between the two visits. I cannot explain it."

Dear reader, neither can anyone else.

It can be hard enough for some office workers to drag themselves into their cubicles every day without the added layer of stress supernatural associations supply. The following account of paranormal problems at the workplace might make annoying coworkers or a short tempered boss look like pleasant alternatives to what awaits employees elsewhere. This account was told to me by the young man who experienced it. He supplied me with ample details regarding this significant event in his life. There is a twist here in that it was the story teller, a person on the outside, who had the more impressive experience and not the one, his young lady friend, actually working at the site in question. His fear for her was greater than hers of the location, but there were more than enough uncomfortable feelings between them for resolve and a little bravery to be required for each to continue their routines concerning the place. A dramatization tells their true tale best. Their names have been changed to protect their privacy.

5
Overtime

Ray walked another block closer to his girlfriend, Cammie's office. Cammie was working in a clerical capacity for a local realtor while learning the business from the inside. Ray always met her at the office when she finished for the day and found the five block walk from the subway pleasant, except, that is, for the last few steps. Those few feet, when the large plate glass store front came into view, always slowed Ray's pace, and no matter how he was feeling a moment ago, always inspired a serious look to spread across his face. Happily, all is well on this day. Inside Ray sees the attractive young lady he has come to meet, the usual desks and chairs and cabinets. For Ray, this is a good day, but he can't help briefly throwing his mind back to another that wasn't.

In the 1990s, Ray and Cammie were two young people living and working in the Astoria neighborhood of Queens, New York. When Ray met Cammie, he was impressed with her positive attitude, an attractive personality trait he felt he shared with her. She was also the kind of young person that was willing to sacrifice some of today to achieve a better tomorrow. Inspired after watching a friend's mother become successful in real estate, she wanted to get into the business herself, and as soon as possible. When she told Ray her plan, he knew she'd find some way to do whatever it took to achieve her goal. Both she and Ray worked, he full time with a local lighting manufacturer, and she part time at a public middle school. That meant Cammie had afternoons free to devote to pursuing her newly targeted field.

Cammie began her career quest by asking her friend's mother questions about being an agent, taking notes, and reading. One day, when Ray came by to take her out for dinner, Cammie had news that had her considerably more excited than their pending dinner date. She was thrilled to announce that she had been able to get a few hours work each afternoon, after her day job, at the offices of a real estate agent in Long Island City. That meant extra money, but what made Cammie so eager to start was the opportunity it afforded her to be close to the Real Estate business on a daily basis. Books and notes were one thing, but to be involved with agents and listings every day in the real world was quite another. The pay was just above minimum wage, but Cammie would have gladly volunteered her time just for the connections and insights she expected to gain. Cammie added that some nights she might be asked to work a little overtime as well as be responsible for locking the place up. That was the one point Ray bristled at. He believed that employees had a duty to put in their hours, but after that, also the right to a full complement of their own time. Cammie reminded him that overtime meant overpaid.

Unmoved, Ray told her he couldn't understand why anyone would choose to linger at their place of work after their duty was done.

They celebrated that evening until a thought occurred to Ray. "Hey," he said, "when am I going to see you if you start this thing?"

"Anytime," she told him. "I quit at six. If you leave your place at five and take the R train, you can be in Long Island City in twenty minutes."

After quickly calculating what the cost of ten subway tokens per week would do to his already tight budget, Ray agreed that the situation didn't change things much. As he asked her questions about her new place of employment, Ray learned that the company Cammie had been hired by was Schoke Real Estate and that they were located on the ground floor of a building on Jackson Avenue. Cammie had been there that day and thought the neighborhood was nice. Ray now knew where he would be spending his future weekday evenings. What one particular such evening would have in store for him was as impossible for Ray to imagine then, as it would be for him to forget later.

A few weeks into his new routine, Ray no longer felt the extra travel time commuting to see Cammie added to his evenings. One particular Friday afternoon, Ray, having clocked out at work, gave Cammie a quick call before heading toward the subway station once again. On the phone, Cammie told Ray she would be ready at the usual time, and that if Ray was early, to wait outside because her boss, Mr. Schoke, was working at the office later than usual. This suited Ray, who always preferred to linger outside until the official company quitting time. He did not like to interrupt the work of others or cause Cammie embarrassment by coming in too early and becoming a distraction. Because Mr. Schoke was usually out of the office by four, Ray had yet to meet Cammie's employer.

This day, as he began his trip, Ray was able to walk onto a waiting train, which took a few minutes off his commute. Additionally, the train was running slightly faster than usual, so Ray neared Cammie's office some minutes ahead of schedule. After his customary trek from the station, Ray approached the storefront windows of the office. Inside he could see Cammie busy on the phone. Normally, he would wave as he went by en route to a time-killing lap around the block until her shift ended, but today he merely glanced in, and then marched on. That was because he observed Mr. Schoke sitting at the desk directly behind Cammie's, shuffling papers and looking rather immersed in his work. The last thing Ray wanted was to make a less-than-professional impression. He would wait until the later, more appropriate time to introduce himself to the gentleman.

As he walked, Ray took in the blue evening sky and enjoyed the mild breeze that filtered through the mostly empty streets. By the time he was back at the corner of Jackson Avenue, he had only to wait there another few minutes before he could enter the office. Soon, Ray thought, another pleasant evening with Cammie would begin, but what happened next would put that, or any future pleasant evenings on hold for some time.

Ray walked the half block to the storefront. Inside Cammie was putting her desk in order and appeared to be the last person left.

Ray pushed the door open and said, "Hey babe."

"Hi," Cammie responded. "I saw you walk by before."

"Yeah," Ray said. "I figured I'd better walk around the block until you were done. The train was early."

"You could have waited in here," Cammie said, scolding slightly. "The minute you went out of sight I was ready to go."

"Sorry," Ray offered. "Anyway, I didn't want to come in here until your boss was gone."

At that, Cammie wrinkled her brow. "What are you talking about?" she asked him.

"I saw your boss was working right behind you." Ray answered with a laugh. "You don't want me to bust in here and get you in trouble, do you?"

Cammie stared at Ray in disbelief. "My boss?" she said. "Nobody else is here. I'm the last one out. I have to lock up."

Now it was Ray's turn to look surprised. "When I walked past here your boss was sitting at his desk right behind you. That's why I walked around the block."

Cammie said, "Ray, are you crazy? I'm the last one here. Mr. Schoke left as soon as I hung up with you. He told me to lock up."

She was beginning to think this was an odd sort of joke for Ray.

"Then who was that sitting behind you?" asked Ray.

Seeing no sign of playfulness in Ray's manner, Cammie raised her voice and said, "Take a look. There isn't even any desk behind mine."

Ray felt a rushing, electric sensation wash over his temples and slither down between his shoulder blades. Goosebumps raised across his skin. For long seconds his mind fought with the evidence of his own eyes. It was true. Ray stared at the empty space where minutes ago he had seen real, solid objects of heft and size.

"Wait a minute," Ray started, still in a fog, "where's the other desk that was right here?"

"I don't know what you're talking about," said Cammie. "There's no desk there. There never was. There isn't even room. Ray, are you kidding me?"

Ray continued to go over the area with his eyes, unable to accept what he saw there. With a small cabinet and low table in the space behind her desk, there was no room for anything else, but he had seen the desk there, and the man sitting behind it, as plainly as he had seen Cammie.

"Are you telling me," Ray said, struggling to understand, "that no desk was here and that no one else was in this office?"

Cammie, starting to become concerned, said sternly, "No!"

"I saw a man sitting at a desk right here!" Ray said insistently, indicating the desk-less space with both hands, "A guy was sitting in a chair, right there, shuffling papers!"

When he turned to look at Cammie for any sign of comprehension, he saw, for the first time, a look of fear marring her young face.

"Ray, don't say that," she said. "I've been hearing things behind me all day! It sounded like somebody else was in here. Ray, it sounded like somebody going through papers!"

At that, the explanation Ray was fishing for tugged his line hard. It distilled itself into a one word declaration that neither spoke, but each heard sounding in their heads like an alarm: "ghost." Tears

were starting to well in Cammie's eyes. Now Ray realized that before he had been confronted with his, Cammie had been managing a mystery of her own that night. The dam she had been building to contain her fears burst against the strain of Ray's story. Ray shifted focus from his own confused feelings to her need for comfort and hugged her.

"All right baby, all right," he said quickly. Reaching for her coat while continuing to hold on to her with one arm, Ray said, "Come on, let's get your stuff and get out of here."

The two young people grabbed the spare keys, hurried out of the building, locked the door, and then paused a few feet away from the building to take deep breaths. The cool, restorative air of the normal world helped exorcise their anxiety. Ray took a long look back at the darkened office interior before they started toward the station. The view of the office from the outside, from where he had observed the apparition, made the absence of the desk and its owner seem even more surreal. Silently he vowed never to let Cammie go back in there again.

Years later after repeatedly and thoroughly going over the scene in his mind, Ray feels he is able to confirm a few details about the vision he witnessed as he walked by the office windows that day. Ray insists he saw a man seated at a desk occupying space that Cammie simultaneously observed to be vacant. He recalls that the phantom desk was large and made of a brown colored wood. Cammie's desk, like the others in the room, was a modern black metal one. Ray is sure that the man wore a white button-down shirt that he describes as having had the look of vintage clothing. He is also convinced he saw a phone on the desk. He describes it as an old model with a straight cord between the base and the receiver, unlike the typical coiled cord of a modern phone of the time. He is sure of that that because it attracted his attention and he kept his eyes on it as he passed by suggesting that the apparition lasted at least as long as it took Ray to walk four or five paces, and could be perceived in three dimensions. As for any possible explanation, if pressed Ray will tell you that, as far as he's concerned, there is only one. He prefers not to elaborate further.

As for Cammie, although she was shaken by the eerie episode, she did go back. She continued to work for the company for months after, even keeping those spare keys and locking up from time to time. On nights when she performed that duty, she would keep her eyes only on the lock until it was bolted, then turn, facing away from the storefront windows, and walk briskly away.

Cammie dealt with the threat of additional contact with whatever was manifesting itself in the office, by consciously deciding to ignore anything odd she might see, hear, or feel going forward. She came to see these incursions as nuisances that had the potential to stand between her and her goal. She decided that any reappearance of the phantom clerk, now that the initial shock had passed, would be something more to be cross with than feared. Fortunately for Cammie, her resolve did not have to be put to the test. Her haunted office coughed up the odd sound now and then, but no new apparitions were seen. Later, when a better opportunity presented itself, Cammie leapt on it, and considered the sense of relief it brought, by taking her away from the supernatural taint of her old office, a definite benefit of her new position.

As previously stated, Cammie is the dedicated type who will do whatever it takes to get the job done and achieve the goal. She is able to put her own personal convenience, even her fears, aside as needs be, and has always believed in things like overtime. Now, in a rather more metaphysical understanding of the term, so does Ray.

6
Push Comes to Shove

Haldeman Mansion: imposing, sprawling, and succumbing to the slow and steady creep of ruin.

Purported to be a most active haunted house, Haldeman Mansion, its outbuildings, and grounds, have been the subject of numerous amateur investigations throughout the years. As a result, the mystique of this storied home has been heightened by the sharing of photographic anomalies and audio aberrations collected there by evidence seeking enthusiasts to the point that even skeptical observers have begun to wonder what exactly is going on there. As the ghost hunters come and go, one brave soul returns night after night as both host to the transient and, she believes, guest of the permanent occupants of the mansion's remains. She is the key holder of that daunting destination whose accounts will either leave you eager to visit, or determined never to set foot inside the historic Haldeman home.

Located at Locust Grove, south of Bainbridge, in Conoy Township, Pennsylvania, the two story stone structure known as the Haldeman Mansion stands facing the Susquehanna River from atop a lonely, grassy rise. From the train that passes the property's edge, and from the river that flows just beyond the tracks, the house presents a neat facade. Modern windows, squared and white, create a sense of order and good repair. In stark contrast, the hollow remains of the spacious rooms inside bear the slights of time, decay, and abandonment. A large fourteen room affair, Haldeman Mansion is comprised of a squared main section and a wing, one-half the width, extending to the rear. An old summer kitchen and a disused sawmill complete the inventory of derelict structures on the property. A monument to the sad reality of success' mortality, the Haldeman family's elegant home, where once were greeted dignitaries of the time, and which was once alive with the activity of large and prosperous families, sits heavily on its ancient foundation, a slain and silent hulk.

Because some of the stories surrounding the mansion are directly connected to the family that lived there for three generations, an overview of who they were in life, before hearing about who, some claim, they continue to be after life, will help to set the table.

The mansion was originally two-thirds smaller when it was built in 1740 by John Gailbraith, part of a family who immigrated to colonial America from Scotland. Then the home was a more modest arrangement of five rooms occupying two stories and which today exists as the rear wing of the mansion. The first Haldeman to arrive in the area was Swiss immigrant Jacob Haldeman. In April of 1741, he was granted a warrant for 100 acres of land. He added to his holdings by purchasing adjoining tracts. He married Maria Miller, and the couple reared twelve children. In later years, Jacob Haldeman bequeathed his estate, in halves, to two of his sons, Abraham and Peter.

The property with the house, which was then known as Locust Grove, was eventually transferred to John Haldeman, another one of Jacob's sons. John was a successful land owner and businessman who, among other things, was involved in the China Trade after the Revolutionary War. He increased his fortune by building a mill and a distillery on the property and by using the nearby Susquehanna River to ferry his goods on their way to market in Philadelphia.

During their stewardship of the estate, John and his wife Mary oversee the enlargement of the original dwelling twice, once in 1798, and again in 1812. These additions account for the large squared section of the house that contains the front parlor, ballroom, and main bedchambers. All that remains of whatever splendor the great home might have had then, is a single mantle and the federal-style staircase that extends from the parlor to the attic. A carved stone set high into an exterior wall commemorates the expansions, and reads, in old German, what translates to, "Erected by John Haldeman and Maria Haldeman 1790." Thus Locust Grove is re-christened the Haldeman mansion. The couple, like old Jacob before them, had twelve children, of which five died during the family's time at the home. In 1813, after a long and fruitful tenancy, the Haldeman Mansion and grounds are transferred to John and Maria's eldest son, Henry.

Henry Haldeman, who was born at the mansion, spent the entirety of his life there. He worked, in association with his brothers, at the family businesses. In 1811, Henry married Frances Stehman. The couple had nine children, only seven of which lived beyond childhood. Frances is known to have loved playing a piano in the great house. She undoubtedly gave lessons to her children, starting with her firstborn, a boy named Sammuel.

Sammuel would be the most renowned member of the Haldeman family by virtue of his accomplishments in natural science and linguistics. Sammuel Stehman Haldeman was born at the mansion in 1812, and lived there until the age of fourteen, at which time he left home and enrolled at an academy in Harrisburg. There he pursued his passion for natural sciences and the study of the historical development of languages. He achieved the position of professor of natural sciences, and later, professor of philology, at the University

of Pennsylvania, and was one of the earliest members of the National Academy of Sciences. So respected was he, that Charles Darwin recognized him for contributions to *The Origin of Species*, and the publishers of *Webster's Dictionary* acknowledged his assistance in supplying information used in the compiling of their reference books. Sammuel Haldeman died in 1880, at which time the mansion had already been sold out of the family.

As this brief overview makes plain, the Haldeman family both valued and took pride in their estate.

Many were born there, some spent a lifetime within its walls, and some drew their last breath, beginning their journey to the next world, from somewhere inside it. A genuine family seat, it is exactly the kind of place anyone with a history there would want to revisit, no matter the circumstances, no matter the obstacles.

Inside the mansion today, there is little left to commemorate the lives that were played out there. Visitors will find a collection of Sammuel's precious artifacts, a few portraits, and an open child's penmanship tablet displaying the morbidly appropriate phrase, "Death is inevitable" carefully inscribed across both pages. There is also a curiously stoic bust of Sammuel, with long pointed beard, carved from a black lusterless stone. No smile is detected, no glint in the eye. He is captured by his portraitist in what could pass for a state of suspended animation, and what more fitting incarnation for the enduring sentinel of a great house forgotten, the last symbol of the presence of the Haldemans. Look in the right window and he'll be there, day or night, expressionlessly surveying you, and the cracked walls and off kilter doors that encase his likeness like a modern-day pyramid protecting its funerary treasure.

There is no lore connected to the smattering of successive owners and caretakers of the mansion that bought, sold, and kept up the property between the last of the Haldemans and its eventual abandonment, but somewhere along the line, for some reason, people lost interest in living there. Since the date of its last transference of ownership in 1963, the mansion has sat vacant for over half a century.

The Haldeman property and house are now under the care of the Haldeman Mansion Preservation Society, an organization whose mission is to restore the building for future use as a museum and educational center. The society's quarterly newsletter lists among its members, Lora Shirey as their recording secretary, but the Upcoming Events section announces that she is also the contact person for a paranormal conference to be held there. She is the society's expert on ghosts.

In this capacity, Lora organizes and brings groups to the mansion for nighttime paranormal investigations. At these events the curious and the courageous roam the rooms of Haldeman, recorders running and cameras at the ready, hoping to see for themselves some of what Lora and others say they have. Voices, tugs, footsteps, banging doors, and sightings have all been checked off Lora's Haldeman list. So, too, has a close encounter that changed the way she conducts her tours and herself when presumed to be in the presence of the mansion's resident spirits.

Clearly, Lora is well versed in the activity at Haldeman, but her introduction to the strange and otherworldly, which led her there, came earlier and elsewhere. In 2002, Lora Shirey was an average, open minded, paranormally detached person occupied with finding a home for herself and her son Drew. Anyone who has hunted for a house knows how stressful it can be as well as appreciate the relief of finally closing on the property that will be your new home. Imagine the impact the statement that follows would have on your peace of mind at such a time. After the legalities were completed, the cowardly seller turned to Lora and said, "Congratulations, your house is haunted."

With no avenue of retreat, the Shireys moved in to the house that would be their home hoping for the best, but preparing for something much less. Their hopeful skepticism was soon rendered moot as the new homeowners experienced proof that their home was indeed going to be a challenge for them. "The activity was mild to begin with." Lora told me, "It started with footsteps and movement of objects, shadows and unexplained noises." Lora managed to coexist with the haunting until an escalation convinced her she needed help. Lora says, "Something started attacking my son. He was repeatedly attacked in his sleep. He would wake up with scratches and bruises, feeling very weak." Eventually, concerned for her son's safety, Lora left the house. She says, "Once we left, it all stopped."

The activity led Lora, a Christian, to seek out religious leaders for answers. Many did not respond and the remainder could offer little in the way of advice. Lora's search for support from that community led her to an unexpected end. She decided that she

would become for others the source of comfort and counseling that she, herself, had been looking for. "I took the liberty of thinking God wanted me to take my experiences and the things I had learned to help other people who had nowhere to turn for help or answers." In 2009, Lora started an investigative team with like-minded members and named it Faith Paranormal.

Sometime later, an acquaintance of Lora's working as a photographer called to discuss the location of her next fashion photo shoot, the formidable Haldeman Mansion. Concerned by the location's reputation and the effect it might have on her models, and herself, the woman asked if Faith Paranormal could do a brief investigation before the day of the shoot. With no specific expectations, the crew walked through the mansion alert for any signs of activity. No evidence of anything that might frighten visitors presented itself until some of the crew came to the basement. An investigator opened the door and began to descend the stairs when he, and everyone with him, heard a voice coming up from the darkened space below. It was the voice of a young girl shouting, "That's Daddy!" After composing themselves, a sweep of the area confirmed what everyone already knew, that no one outside the group was present in the mansion, let alone the crumbling, catacomb-like basement. What they had heard was distinct, loud, young, female, and, apparently, other-than-flesh-and-blood in origin. It was an impressive catch.

The experience prompted Lora to propose to the Preservation Society board that she be given the chance to bring funding to the mansion in a new, somewhat different, way. She volunteered to preside over paranormal investigations of the property, bringing more, exciting publicity to the site, and $60 a head to the coffers. The board of directors, considered, voted on, and approved the suggestion, ultimately presenting her with her own key. Lora Shirey and the Haldeman Mansion were officially joined.

For Lora, ghosts were now her business, and business was good. Groups enthusiastically responded to the mansion's offer to host investigations. Lora informed and guided visiting teams, sometimes removing herself to the break room allowing free rein, and other times joining guests eager to have an experienced mentor close at hand. According to Lora, there was no shortage of ghostly experiences, and as the weeks and months passed, a steady accumulation of potential evidence began to take shape. Lora recognized patterns in the phenomena and, by studying the known traits of the previous inhabitants, began to associate certain activity in certain areas with specific figures from the mansion's past. The list included Native Americans who had been sighted on the grounds, and, naturally, members of the Haldeman family. Some of the supposed spirits in visitation at the mansion include two male presences who are confined to the basement, a young boy and girl that appear throughout the house playing in tattered clothing and who are sometimes heard giggling, a troubled teen named Jacob, and even a phantom cat. Among the recorded evidence are unidentified voices and baffling snippets of piano music. Needless to say, there has not been an instrument of any kind kept at the mansion for decades. Lora postulates that the sounds might be linked to Frances Haldeman, Henry's wife, who enjoyed playing the piano during her time as a living sojourner at the, then, well-appointed abode. Henry himself is credited as being the ill-tempered spirit that claims the ballroom as his particular domain. Visitors complain of an unseen male entity who comes up behind them and exhales sharply close to their ear. For Lora's money, that's Henry's modus operandi. Henry is also present in the artifact room, a place that houses an original archeological collection of native relics unearthed on the property by Sammuel. Lora sees Henry as a short-tempered, controlling spirit. She claims no special sensitivity, but states that it is not uncommon for her to feel agitated, as if by osmosis, as soon as she enters Henry's ballroom. On one occasion she says," I just wanted to jump up and down cussing every word in the book—and I don't cuss!" One Faith team member earned everyone's attention during an investigation when he suddenly cried out in pain while standing in the artifact room. He complained of being jabbed in the midsection, and when he lifted his shirt, his comrades observed harsh red marks on his skin, any source for which they were at a loss to discover. The ghosts of Haldeman Mansion speak as well. With the use of electronic enablers, Lora and her teams have heard the man in the ballroom presumably tell other spirits to "Be quiet" and to "Go upstairs." A voice attributed to Frances was captured saying, "Watch the back stairs," which was taken to be a warning against Henry's movements and his foul moods.

In her role as the mansion's proctor, Lora hosts guests with a variety of interest levels, and acknowledges that some para-investigators simply "do it for the thrill." The aftermath of such thrills usually acts to separate these types from more serious evidence seekers. For example, Lora once had a small group of no-nonsense, off-duty narcotics agents as guest investigators. Curious, but doubtful of being frightened by the mansion's ghost stories, these burly specimens and their wives swaggered through Lora's tour. Half-way up the stairs to the second floor, their bravado was quickly jettisoned when something was felt dashing by them so quickly, and with such force, it pasted both men against the wall in shock. Their wives spent the rest of their evenings waiting in their cars content to think of their sixty dollar fees as charitable donations for which no further compensation was required.

Some no doubt envy Lora's unlimited access to her paranormal hot spot, but besides being allowed to stay all night, guests may also leave anytime they feel uncomfortable. That is one luxury Lora cannot claim. I asked her if it ever happened that she had to take groups into the house when she wasn't prepared for another supernatural soiree. She answered that that had happened frequently, and that at such times her vulnerability would manifest itself as dizziness, shortness of breath, and headaches. Fear was less of a factor, and the more time Lora spent at the mansion, the more accustomed to all that is not ordinary with the location she became. Being the emcee of a haunted mansion was working to the point where Lora had mechanisms to deal with almost anything the other side could hand out, but, as with most mechanisms, at some point they all need a little adjustment.

One night, when Lora was hosting a group of investigators at Haldeman, she had her son, Drew, now a young man, and who had yet to see the mansion, join her there. Leaving her guests in the house, Lora took Drew to the Summer Kitchen, the oldest building on the property. The kitchen building is believed to house a female spirit who is always in residence and who will touch male visitors on the back of their heads or even, on occasion, sing to let people know that she is with them. In that place, in anticipation of that

kind of encounter, Lora and Drew would seek evidence of their own. Using her key, Lora opened the door, let her son inside, and then closed it behind them. Although Lora brought her flashlight, the two chose to perform their vigil in darkness, Drew in a chair and Lora with her back to the rear wall. After a time marked by inactivity, Lora decided to provoke a response by challenging any reluctant astral company with statements like, "You don't scare me" and "I'm not afraid of you." The ploy apparently worked, because soon after the pair could hear footsteps on the second story floor above them. With the guest investigators in the main house, and having had to unlock the door to get in, they were sure no living person was pacing the loft overhead. Lora asked Drew if he heard the sounds. When he said that he did, Lora urged the spirit to continue by saying that she was not impressed by the booming upstairs. "Why don't you come downstairs?" she called up. "I'm not afraid of you!" To their amazement, the footsteps, rather than stopping or continuing unchanged, began to make their way across the loft and down the stairs, in direct response to Lora's dismissive invitation. A definite element of apprehension crept into the scene. Lora decided not to wait to see what might happen next and, taking Drew with her, instinctively vacated the building in haste. The intense manifestation had exceeded either's expectations of the Summer Kitchen.

Lora was relieved to be outside until her son commented, "Wow, I've never seen you run from anything!" The young man's comment hit a chord. Lora had been her son's protector in the early days of their dealings with these kinds of things, and she did not want her son's confidence in that role to be weakened. Steeling herself, she escorted Drew back into the pitch-dark building and closed the door behind them once more. Again they took seats, this time next to one another, backs snug against the rear wall so that they were both facing the door. The slim gap between the bottom of the door and the ground outside was illuminated by moonlight. Lora worked up as much outward bravery as she could while inwardly her heart pounded in protest. The desire to not let her son feel the fear she fought to keep under control prompted her to continue the aggressive barrage of taunts. "You're not going to scare me out of here. I'm back." She declared, "Bring it on." Soon, each became aware of movement disturbing the slit of pale light under the door. Any person or animal outside would cast shadows that taper and vary in intensity as they move back and forth. These were not like that, in fact they were not shadows at all. These were solid dark shapes that did not vary in density as they crisscrossed the narrow moonlight gap. Whatever was responsible for the weird movement was not outside, but inside the room. As they watched the darting shapes, Lora and Drew heard no accompanying sound disturb the stillness of the small space. It seemed possible to Lora that the spirit that had previously boomed down the staircase had remained on the ground floor and was now sizing up its mortal antagonizers. Eventually the movement stopped. The next things Lora experienced were touches to the back of her head, slight pressures that she attributed to the female spirit who usually only makes such contact with men. Although out of character, Lora assumed the spirit was interacting with her in angry reaction to her earlier antagonistic demands. Then Lora felt a hard pressure at the back of her head that actually caused her to move forward. Disconcerted, but maintaining her veneer of calm for Drew's sake, she shrugged it off and said nothing. The encounter continued, and soon Lora felt some one touching her right arm. Believing it was Drew, she turned to respond to him. It had not been Drew. With her eyes having adjusted somewhat to the dark, she could see enough of his form to tell that Drew was no longer sitting directly beside her. He had turned so that now his back was facing her. Curious as to what could have taken his attention away from the area under the door, Lora moved her gaze to the corner of the room to their right. Now she, too, had to re-focus her attention. Against the wall, defined by a soft white light was a distinct, if featureless, human form. She describes a well-defined head, neck and shoulders terminating into a mass representing the vision's body. Lora describes the effect as of something made of "encased" light, but emitting none. No area around the apparition showed evidence of being illuminated by it. Then came the vibe. Lora says, "You could feel the energy, and I could tell that whatever that was, it was very angry with me." Needing no additional incentive, Lora and Drew rose and went out of the building. They had been brave and had stood their ground long enough. Now it was time to ponder what had just happened at a safer distance and leave the Summer Kitchen and its contents behind.

Years after the fact, as we sat in the kitchen building going over her story, Lora told me, "It took me a long time to come back in here." Anyone would be able to relate to her confession after hearing what happened that night, but one of the reasons for that prolonged absence had nothing at all to do with a fear of returning. One of the results of Lora's provocation session, and the shove she received in response, was a long hospital stay and recovery period from what her doctors described as trauma to the head. After her experience in the Summer Kitchen, Lora began to suffer stroke-like symptoms and ended by spending three months in a state of partial paralysis. Physicians gave her treatments and advised her on how to go forward after recovery from her brain injury, but not one of them could explain how she had received it in the absence of a physical blow. All Lora can testify to is that the only contact she had to her head was the pressure and shove delivered by unseen hands in the Haldeman Summer Kitchen. She had not been involved in any accidents prior to, or after that event. It is safe to assume that any alternate cause would have presented itself to her doctors during the time she was in their care.

Lora still suffers some effects of her illness, but perhaps an even greater effect has been leveled at her approach to how she interacts with the energies that cross her path in haunted places.

In order to adapt to her immersion in paranormally active locations, particularly the Haldeman house, Lora has developed a code of behavior and a philosophy concerning how she understands the presences she is likely to encounter. Lora's advice for anyone planning to venture into a haunted location is based on common decency and sense. "If you ask respectfully rather than demand," Lora insists, "they'll interact with you more. The nicer you are to them, the more you are going to get back." She says, "If they are mean or nasty, or in a bad mood, they're people, and you have to respect their feelings the same way you want them to respect yours." Lora also suggests, "You have to remember they are from another time. Put yourself back in their day and behave appropriately." She condemns provocation and adds, "Use proper language, don't curse, and don't talk about controversial things that might offend (people of another time)." By the same token, Lora believes in not being bullied. She says, "I'm not afraid to go up against them. If they do something to anger me, I'm going to go back at them." Lora believes, as do many others in her field, that fear only encourages more mischievous or negative responses. Aside from all her respectfulness and fearlessness, Lora also feels safer going into situations with a little protection, which, for her, is provided by her faith. "I'm definitely here for a reason," Lora says. "This is what God wants me to do. I believe that our journeys are laid out for us." With resolve, Lora accepts the strange journey laid out for her, and navigates it one hard-learned step at a time hoping the major perils along her dark, uncharted path are finally behind her.

Lora's experience at Haldeman Mansion taught her something about the boundaries between the world she sees and the one she only sometimes glimpses. She sees them both as worlds populated by human beings who share common desires to be recognized, to be respected and, ultimately, to be left in peace. As long as she can rely on that basic tenet, Lora will continue to guide her guests through the great house by the Susquehanna. She'll hang on to that key.

Before I leave this tale, I have one last supportive fact that I must impart. As I went about organizing materials for my chapter on Lora and the Haldeman Mansion, I listened to tracks on my digital recorder and took notes. While reviewing track number three, I listened to Lora describe, as we walked through the Haldeman ballroom, how the spirit of Henry Haldeman, the ghost with the belligerent streak, has a penchant for coming up to people and breathing hard close to their ear in order to frighten them. I had to chuckle and shake my head. Forty seconds before she is heard making that claim there is an unexplained sound on my digital recorder. I assure you, neither Lora nor I paused to make it or heard it at the time of our walk. We would have certainly remarked upon it if we had. It is the very distinct sound of a male voice exhaling long and harshly in what would have been the relative proximity of my ear.

7
Encore

There are those in society who willingly possess the keys to haunted places that the majority of us would sooner have nothing to do with. A certain intestinal fortitude, and a compunction to not be chased away, arms them for a daily test of wills they have determined not to lose. That is their choice, and it is admirable. Alternately, there are others among us who are unwittingly presented with such keys for temporary possession, and who, vulnerable in innocence, are often subject to the full force of the unwelcome experiences they unlock.

Marie Danvers' career has been long and rewarding, but at times she has found herself, by virtue of her profession, at perilous odds with creatures of the night. One such opponent was none other than Erik, the scarred and bitter villain better known as the Phantom of the Opera! Marie explains, "I had the privilege of playing Christine Daae on Broadway, as well as in the national tour of *Phantom*." Now a professor of theatre arts at Five Towns College in Dix Hills, New York, Marie spent the first thirty years of her career working as an equity actor, achieving leading roles in such productions as *West Side Story*, *A Chorus Line*, and the *Mikado*. Other career highlights include performing with Robert Goulet in tours of the *Fantasticks*, and being part of the cast of television's *As the World Turns*. Marie's husband, Rob, is also an actor with Broadway credentials of his own. Her impressive resume creates a picture of a life punctuated by excitement, but there has been more than one kind of excitement highlighting the actress's days on stage and on the road. She reflects on one particular part of her past with no less interest than her triumphs, but with, perhaps, a bit less cheer.

In discussing her childhood as prologue to her story, Marie informed me that she grew up in a household that openly embraced the concept of the spirit world, as well as that of its inhabitants' ability to contact and influence the living. Discussions centering on paranormal phenomena were not uncommon in her family of believers, and in that environment of acceptance, Marie developed a level of belief of her own regarding the idea of a spirit life after death. One remarkable moment she will never forget was being told, when she was still very young, that she was the reincarnation of her father's sister, an aunt who had died early in life. The extraordinary claim was made to Marie's father by a medium and was not entirely discouraged by her family members.

"I grew up with all of that in my head," Marie told me, making the point that her early days were colored by a one-sided narrative that favored belief.

Later in her life, after the passing of her father, a man she describes as having had psychic abilities, she prepared herself for spiritual contact from him. She felt sure that if anyone on the other side would want to, and could reach her, it would be he. But instead of affirmation, Marie was given reason to doubt as days, and then weeks, passed by without so much as a sign. That disappointment began to erode her convictions, and an attraction to skepticism began to challenge all the faith her family had heretofore instilled. Marie still wonders at times, in the face of anything potentially psychic or paranormal in nature, if her perception isn't biased by her unusual upbringing. Now, she always respectfully defaults first to her skeptical side, preferring to try to debunk anything difficult to explain. If that courtesy fails to deliver a satisfactory answer, however, Marie must then default to the evidence of her senses. Sometimes, as in the case that follows, that evidence suggests that skepticism might, on occasion, be the stretch.

It was a winter in the late 1980s when Marie found herself touring the country with a musical theatre company. The show the group was bringing to audiences, on their five-month trek across the nation, was Rodgers and Hammerstein's *The King and I*. It was Marie's second tour since leaving college, so she was well prepared for life on the road, where one's home is a hotel room occupied for one week, or three days, or two at a time. Another difference between this and her first tour was the fact that Marie had graduated from an ensemble member to a leading role. Her roommate, a young lady who Marie described as "a super talented lady" and as a "good friend at the time" was also playing a lead, so the two had much to talk about when retiring to their room at the end of a long day. After the night featured in the following account, they would be able to discuss a good deal more.

The unusual part of Marie's story began when the traveling troupe arrived in Spokane, Washington, for a two-day stopover. Upon arrival at their hotel, an establishment which shall remain nameless for our purposes, Marie and her roommate each received keys to the two-bed accommodation they would be calling home for the next two nights. The room was small, but comfortable, with a large window looking out over the Spokane River, high efficiency heating, and a modern 27" television. For young performers, hotel rooms, as long as they are clean and in a safe part of town, are the least of their concerns, and the talented pair immediately focused on getting to the local theatre to get the lay of the stage and start rehearsal. Their day was a hurried, but structured, routine culminating in what could surely be described as a dream come true for aspiring young actresses, plying their craft as professionals before an appreciative audience. After a day that included travel, show prep, performing, and all the business that comes after, sleep would come easily to Marie and her colleague. Marie could have sworn on her way to their hotel that night that nothing on earth could get her head off that pillow once she was ensconced in her soft, warm bed.

After going over the pros and cons of the night's performance, the two young actresses pulled the curtains shut, turned off the lamp that stood on a small table between the beds, and settled down for some much needed rest. The hotel linens were soft, and the low rush of warm air from the heating unit doubled as soothing background noise for drifting off to sleep. For a while, Marie lay awake, unable to drift off as easily as she had predicted. As time passed, the silence from her roommate's side of the room inferred that she had had no such difficulty. At the time, Marie attributed no significance to her inability to immediately find rest. In the early stages of the night, she remembers going in and out of sleep as people sometimes do when they are restless, or are disturbed by noises or movement in or outside their room. Marie recalls feeling drowsy, but definitely being awake at times throughout the night, with eyes opened, seeing the shadowy forms of the objects around her in the hotel room and hearing the heater run.

On one of the occasions when she momentarily awakened, Marie remembers noticing that the room felt much cooler than it had when she had gone to bed. She was slightly chilled in spite of the fact that she was snug under the bedding. Although Marie had felt warm air being emitted by the heater before retiring, she concluded the thermostat must have been set too low, by the housekeepers who serviced their room, to counter the outside temperature. She was slightly uncomfortable, but not wanting to get up to make the adjustment, Marie gathered the sheet and bedspread more tightly around her against the cold and attempted to return to sleep. Some time passed, and Marie again found herself awakened, gazing at the walls and drawn curtains of her temporary lodgings while on her side on the bed. Again she was aware of the chill of cold air in the room, only this time the temperature drop was more severe. Now the cold was harsh and penetrating, and Marie knew no amount of shifting under her blankets would do to fend it off. The heater continued to blow warm air into the darkened room, but apparently to no effect. Marie began to wonder if something external might be contributing to the unusually damp, frigid atmosphere. Something about the way the cold felt, and beyond that, the general feeling in the room, was, for want of a better word, unnatural. What happened next confirmed that suspicion in dramatic fashion.

Forced back to a semi-wakefulness a third time, presumably by the extreme cold, Marie became aware of an unexpected sensation. She felt a heaviness along the length of her body. From her feet to her neck, Marie was aware of a weight that she could not attribute to anything on the bed. Then, unbelievably, Marie felt her body start to slowly sink under pressure from above into the now cold mattress of her bed. Staying still, she felt the force eventually level off, hold, and then stop. Fully awake now, and frightened, Marie kept her eyes shut. In this way, she was unable to see anything, and she heard no sounds; but in spite of that, Marie sensed something like the presence of another person in the room. Without any sensory prompts to guide her, Marie nonetheless felt that the presence was that of a man, and an imposing one at that. Marie lay on her left side in the bed, her head sideways on the pillow. Now on the alert for any suggestion of movement, she remained motionless in that position and waited.

Before long, Marie felt that the person who had pushed down on her, and who was still hovering nearby, was lowering himself toward her again. She was convinced that the male presence was moving his face closer to hers and preparing to whisper something into her ear. Marie somehow, perhaps psychically, became certain his intention was to impart a message. Soon, Marie says, she could feel the nearness of the man's lips, could feel warmth as if from his breath against her cold ear. While she struggled to comprehend what was happening and how to react, a warning came to Marie through the fog of her fear. She became convinced that the intruder's message would be somehow unbearable, that more than anything, she must prevent the entity, now poised to speak, from putting those words, whatever they were, into her ear. Armed with that resolve, she willed her eyes open and lifted herself on the bed. "There it was," Marie said, "standing next to me on my right."

What Marie saw she describes as an apparition of a tall, broad-shouldered man clad in a long, tattered overcoat. His garment was similar to a western duster, and not of recent vintage. The figure was visible to Marie despite the fact that there was no source of light in the room which could have illuminated him. The figure appeared slightly fluorescent. She detected no features on the man's darkened face, but saw long tresses of black hair that hung about his head.

Either the figure's appearance, or some other, more subtle aspect projected by it, made Marie believe that the figure was that of a Native American. One final detail that made the scene even more unreal was the fact that, according to Marie, the figure, his clothes, and his long hanks of hair were all soaking wet and dripping as he stood by the bed. For the moment she observed him, Marie felt the figure exuded a feeling of anguish or suffering, but also felt that he projected no anger toward her. "He was just looking through me," Marie told me. "Then I realized I could see through him to the wall on the other side."

As if the strange pressure and the appearance of the apparition were not enough of a show of paranormal prowess, the exiting of the tall man in the soaking cloak was twice as bizarre as his entrance. Marie describes what she witnessed in the space of a second. "The man turned and left in the direction of the foot of my bed," she says. "I heard a ticking noise, *tick, tick, tick*, as he moved out of the room." The sounds came in rapid succession and did not resemble footsteps or any other identifiable human sound. The most intriguing aspect

of the departure was what Marie describes as a second manifestation that inexplicably appeared. "He moved out of the room through some kind of glass door. On the other side of the door I could see water in the distance, like a lake." An instant later, the vision was gone and where the glass door with the lake landscape beyond it had been, now was the blank hotel wall a few yards across from the bed. The episode was over.

Marie swiftly turned and felt for the switch on the bedside lamp. When the light came on, her roommate, who, to Marie's surprise, was awake and sitting up in her bed, asked her what was going on. Marie, still feeling the effects of the terrifying interlude, asked if the other girl had seen or heard anything. She replied that she had not, but that she was awakened from sleep by the extreme cold. Marie excitedly told her roommate everything she had experienced moments ago. Unlike a dream, the sequence of the events and the mental images she had of them were clear, and she was able to recount everything in explicit detail. The two tried to make sense of Marie's story, but short of a bad dream or hallucination, no explanation for the cold, the pressure, or any of the phenomena presented itself. Her roommate told Marie that she believed in such things and believed her story, especially in light of the fact that she experienced the extreme temperature fluctuations herself. It was then that the two noticed that the air in the room was once again a pleasant seventy degrees. Somehow, the biting cold had evaporated the instant Marie's night visitor had vanished through his portal. Eventually the two succumbed to exhaustion and slept without further incident until morning. Needless to say, the lamp on the table between their beds burned all night.

The next morning, the two friends told the other members of the company the amazing facts about the ghost who had appeared to Marie in their room. Their co-workers listened in rapt amazement not knowing what to make of the unreal sounding account. It wasn't until Marie unfolded her story to a hotel employee that she gained any insight as to why the incident in her room happened, and why it was likely to happen again. The person connected to the hotel assured Marie that she was not the first guest to have a ghostly encounter within the walls of the building. She revealed that she had heard many such stories during her years there. She humbly confirmed that the hotel was genuinely, thoroughly, haunted.

With one more night on tap for the anxious pair, that was the last thing they wanted to hear, but the show must go on, and they bravely hunkered down for their second night a little better prepared if somewhat worse for wear. To their relief, the second night passed without incident, and the following morning Marie returned her key to the front desk with the kind of relief one experiences when returning a rattlesnake after pet sitting one for a friend.

If the story ended there, it would be strange enough, but the "other side" had not finished with Marie and her family yet. Years after Marie's encounter with the Native American spirit, her husband Rob found himself on a tour of his own. For Rob's company, the show was the long running musical based on Victor Hugo's novel *Les Miserables*, and popularly known as *Les Miz*. On the road, and sleeping in a hotel room of his own one night, Rob was troubled by a nightmare in which he saw what he described as a hooded figure. Awakened in the middle of the night, presumably by the dream, Rob opened his eyes to see a silhouette of what appeared to be a person in hooded garb standing next to his bed in the darkened room. Startled, Rob bolted upright in the bed and as he did, the figure made a bizarre exit. Rob describes what he saw as the figure seeming to be "peeled away" from the bottom up, in a motion such as one would use to remove tape from a pane of glass. Eventually, after the shock of witnessing the figure subsided enough, Rob was able to sleep again, but his rest would not last long. Rob was awakened a second time during the night, during which he, like Marie before him, experienced an extreme temperature drop. The comfortable air of a moment ago was replaced with an icy cold that permeated the room. The chilling sensation was coupled with an even more disturbing one. Also as Marie had experienced years ago, Rob felt his body being pressed into the bed by an unseen force that weighed down across the entirety of his body. In response, Rob turned himself hard on the bed, as if to push the source of the downward thrust away. He succeeded in ending the frightening episode, but needless to say, he was on the alert for the remainder of that night, and any rest he was able to salvage from his evening was not of the deep, restorative kind.

The following morning, when Rob related his story to the others traveling with him, he was surprised to hear that he was not the only one in the group to have paranormal problems during the night. A friend, whose wife and two sons were traveling with him, reported seeing an apparition in his room as well. He told Rob of how he was awakened late at night by feeling some sort of movement on the bed. Opening his eyes, he saw his wife standing over one of the couple's two young boys. When he asked if everything was all right, the woman he believed to be his wife vanished into thin air. Looking toward the other bed in the room, he found his wife lying there fast asleep. Who it was he had seen standing at the foot of the child's bed he could not say, to where or how she departed he could not explain.

Interested in what the hotel staff would have to say about such activity, the men retold their stories to the clerk at reception. He listened politely and with genuine interest but exhibited none of the surprise the actors thought sure their tales would inspire. After a respectful pause, the clerk told them that he had heard such claims before, and that he was sorry, but the gentlemen might have to expect that kind of thing any time they spend a night in the hotel. He informed them that, besides affording picturesque views of the Spokane River, the hotel was, unfortunately, haunted. A call to Marie confirmed Rob's suspicion. The troupe had spent the night in the same Washington hotel that hosted Marie's years ago. The remarkable coincidence, coupled with the extraordinary events each had experienced at the location, prompted Rob to research the history of the hotel in an attempt to understand why it had such strange effects on its guests. In the short time he had in town, Rob was able to visit the local library and read some accounts of the history of the area that included the site of the hotel. He learned that, in the 1800s, native tribes occupied the land around the Spokane River and the nearby Four Lakes region. Conflicts in the area between the native peoples and the United States infantry came to a head in 1858, after the massacre of a regiment by a force of over 1,000 Native Americans that included members the Spokan tribe. In response, General George Wright led a counter offensive of equal force, but better armed, and handed the tribes a terrible defeat. Battles in the area left thousands on both sides dead, transforming the land into a mass of unmarked graves and the site of many sudden, violent deaths.

Besides helping to explain why restless spirits might be populating the area, the information supports Marie's impression that the apparition she saw was a Native American, and even hints as to why he was seen drenched and retreating into a landscape that included a large body of water. Battles between the warring factions often took place around the lakes and rivers that are found there. One would like to think that the loss of life is a high enough cost to accept for resolving hostilities with violence. If, over one hundred and fifty years later, some victims of conflict still seek solace, or revenge, or recognition from their survivors, how truly terrible might that cost be?

Although Marie admits the experience at the Spokane hotel "scared the hell out of me," in hindsight, she wishes she had had the courage to listen to the message the apparition in the hotel room sought to deliver to her. For some reason she cannot quite explain, she has long felt a sort of psychic affinity for the native peoples of America. As far as ever returning to the hotel, Marie says she would, which is a testament to her bravery. Considering the scene that played out in her room those many years ago, I am sure few in her profession would care to return for an encore.

One last piece of the puzzle is worth relating before leaving Marie's story. Years after her experiences at the hotel in Spokane, Marie was visiting Paris, France. While riding in an elevator there, a man, a complete stranger, approached her and told her, in all earnestness, that he had known Marie in a past life. That in itself, although out of the ordinary, adds little to the discussion about Marie's Washington encounter, until you consider that there was a reason she was able to understand the man without a translator. You see, he was not a Frenchman, or even European. The man who claimed to have past knowledge of Marie was, like her, a visitor from the States. He did not mention from which of the states he hailed, only that his family had a long, long history in the country. He was, he claimed, the last in a long line of full-blooded Native Americans.

8
Tiny Bubbles

During the time I spent listening to people's stories about the active places they spend, or spent, their time in every day, I found out that there are as many different strategies for dealing with their frequent paranormal encounters as there are people frequently encountering them. I made the acquaintances of skeptics, believers, and some perplexedly puzzled people taking stances somewhere in the fuzzy middle. I listened as contributors offered, as bona fide evidence, accounts of apparitions, telekinetic forces, disembodied voices, and even physical abuse. Perhaps the most unique description of a phenomena observed at a supposedly haunted location came from a lady who witnessed a manifestation, perhaps less frightening, but no less unusual, or less of a challenge to explain than any other, while working at the hotel that was her home away from home for over twenty five years.

In compliance with her wishes, and those of the current management of the hotel, I will present the facts of the case, and dramatize the events associated with it, based upon my interviews but using fictitious names and locations. Neither party seeks publicity.

For your consideration, then, I present the following version of their story which I have chosen to call "Tiny Bubbles." Anyone familiar with popular music of the sixties will instantly be reminded of the song of the same name recorded by Don Ho. In his tribute to the charms of champagne, Mr. Ho sings, "Tiny bubbles, make me warm all over." You might find our subject's story odd, even amusing, but these tiny bubbles will never be accused of making anyone feel warm all over.

Like many residents of the neighborhood of Central Pittsburg, Patricia H. had heard legends concerning the stately Rand Hotel well before she applied to become a part of it. Also like those many residents, she had never spent any time working or residing at the hotel prior to her employment there, so legends were all she believed them to be. Among people from the area there was a vague belief that the place was haunted, presumably due to a murder or suicide. More likely is the explanation that the building was simply very old and possessed of an imposing façade that made it seem anachronistic, and consequently a bit out of place, between its more modern neighbors. So it was that Patricia's only reaction to finding out that she would be joining the staff of the local landmark as reception clerk was gladness and a sense of relief that her search for employment was at an end.

The first days at her new position were marked by training, tips, and generally settling in while getting to know the other members of the hotel staff. Patricia heard a lot about the hotel's amenities, its history, and its goals for the future, but not a word about its alleged haunting made it into any of those early conversations.

A few weeks into her assignment at the front desk, Patricia made the acquaintance of two of the cleaning staff who had come by to empty trash and tidy the reception area during a lull in their regular duties, maintaining the rooms on the eleventh floor. They were Clara, the senior of the two, and Cathy. Their conversation was polite and general, with the two woman from housekeeping inquiring as to how Patricia was faring while learning the ropes, and taking time to fill her in on the maintenance policies regarding the front desk and lobby. Eventually, Patricia casually asked the pair how their day was progressing.

"Fine," said Clara. "Just dog tired as usual."

"I'll bet," Patricia replied with a half-smile and a nod denoting sympathy. "You both must work so hard."

"Yeah," said the other. "Well at least nothing weird happened today."

Patricia, at a loss, threw the word back, "Weird?"

Clara looked at Patricia with a quizzical scrunch of her brow and said, "Didn't they tell you about this place?"

Cathy grinned and let out a short, telling "Hmm!" Patricia said that she hadn't heard anything about the hotel that wasn't ordinary or expected.

Her co-worker from the eleventh floor filled her in, "This place is haunted."

That was the first time since her arrival that she was reminded of the inglorious reputation the hotel had on the outside. Unsure if they were as serious as they appeared to be, or just teasing the newcomer, Patricia asked them to elaborate.

She had been introduced to the hotel's public image by her supervisors, now she would hear the other history of her new place of employment. She learned from her new friends that over the years the hotel had been home to many happy and loyal employees. These longtime associates had provided decades of service to the hotel, and so became well known and liked by many of the other employees. Most had retired, but some, unfortunately, had passed while still in the employ of their beloved hotel. Patricia was told that housekeepers assigned to the upper floors of the Rand report occasionally seeing people, in rooms they know to be vacant, and that they describe as being the images of some of their departed co-workers. Also, sometimes, Patricia was told, guests checked into rooms on floors ten, eleven, and twelve, will report seeing strangers in their rooms whose descriptions paint pictures of the same long gone employees. No one ever sees where they go. They seem to simply disappear.

"And that's not all," added Cathy. "You should hear what happens to me! Sometimes I'll be cleaning a room up there and things will happen. Crazy stuff!" Cathy, having claimed the floor, continued, "Like the sheets on the bed. I always make the beds first, then I go in the bathrooms. Then, when I come out, sometimes the comforters and all the pillows are just flung on the floor—after I just put them up! And I know nobody comes in there and does it because I would hear them."

She looked at Patricia and asked, "How do you explain that?"

"I can't," Patricia said.

"And what about seeing them in the windows?" Clara interjected.

"Oh, don't even talk to me about that," Cathy replied. "I don't even look up there anymore."

When Patricia asked Cathy why she wouldn't look up at the hotel windows, the woman shook her head and said, "I've seen people looking out those windows that I know weren't." She emphasized, "*regular* people." She explained, "There was this one woman, Marie . . ."

"Marie Tasse," Clara clarified.

Cathy continued, "She, Marie Tasse, used to rent the ballroom at Christmas every year. She was always around here, everybody knew her. Well, she dies a few years ago, maybe four or five. So, I'm leaving work one night, and for some reason I feel like I should turn around and look back at the building. I turn, and I swear on my mother's grave, I see Marie looking out of the second floor window!" Cathy closed her eyes and, after a few rapid shakes back and forth of her head, said, "I can see it right now. It was the creepiest thing."

Patricia, having just heard the claims about the hotel, instinctively reached for an explanation. "Are you sure," she asked, "it wasn't just a guest that maybe looked like her?"

"There was nobody there," Clara chimed in. "It was last Christmas and no one was in that room. She checked, right?" she said addressing Cathy.

Cathy answered, "I checked. I thought I was going crazy so the next day I checked if anyone was in that room and they said no."

"And there were other people that saw ghosts in the windows too." Clara added, "They saw people that used to work here looking right out the windows."

Although the woman did their best to convince Patricia that the hotel was indeed a haunted one, she remained skeptical. These kinds of claims one needs to see for oneself to really believe. Patricia soon forgot about the stories as her day began to demand her full attention.

That evening, on her way out, Patricia walked as far as under the entrance awning before cognizance of her location recalled to her mind her earlier talk with Clara and Cathy. Realizing she was standing in front of the building, she wondered if there would be any point in looking back to the second story windows, just to see for herself if there was anything sinister about them. She looked, and saw only rows of vacant glass rectangles reflecting the fiery light of the setting sun. There was no one staring out at the living below, just as she knew there would not be. Still, a minor shiver tingled between her shoulders at the thought of the alternative, forcing her to physically shrug the feeling off. She recalled Cathy's claim regarding the bedclothes that fly off the beds on the eleventh floor, looked higher, in that floor's direction, and wondered, if their stories are true, how do those women manage to keep going up there? Glad she had no such troubles, Patricia turned and headed home.

Several years had passed between the time of her hiring and those initial conversations with the hotel's true believers, to the time of the events that would constitute Patricia's personal brush with one of the strange manifestations the old Rand Hotel had to offer. During those years, Patricia continued to hear second-, and third-hand accounts of apparitions being seen by guests and staff. These stories interested her, but she continued to vacillate between crediting them and rejecting them as cases of overexcited imaginations, or as pranks. Patricia never felt any apprehension about being in the building day after day herself, because she had never heard of anything happening to anyone in the lobby or other areas she frequented during a typical day. Even if the claims were true, they appeared to be confined to the upper regions of the hotel, and Patricia came to think of her assigned territory an unofficial safe haven. As it turned out, she rarely saw Clara or Cathy, and felt silly asking about any possible new experiences they might have to report on when she did. For her, the entire subject eventually became nothing more than a background curiosity, a localized conundrum for others to sort out, but not her.

Patricia's "safe haven" was the most spacious and open part of the hotel. From the counter, where Patricia and her co-workers in reception were situated, there is a clear view of the guest sitting areas to the left and right of the main aisle that leads to reception from the front door. These open areas feature large plate glass windows that let in an abundance of natural light while affording wide views of the street activity in front of the building. The east and west hallways are entirely visible from the reception counter and include a recessed computer station, the conference rooms, the two elevator stations and, at the extreme ends of each, steel doors with pebbled acrylic window insets, behind which are found the stairways going to the upper floors. Although she was not confined to her counter all day, Patricia spent the better part of most of them dealing with guests from it, so that the landscape of the lobby and hallways was as familiar to her as the rooms of her own home. She could probably have navigated them with her eyes shut, and would surely have noticed anything different or out of place immediately. On two occasions, she did just that.

One day, in the latter hours of a slow, early spring morning, Patricia was manning the front desk alone. She divided her time between attending to the odd guest and thumbing vacation brochures she had picked up in preparation for her summer trip. During one long free moment, Patricia noticed movement, or something, from the corner of her right eye. She folded her pamphlet and looked down the west hallway expecting to see an approaching guest or supervisor. She was surprised to see the hallway empty of people, but something was there that caught her eye. Barely visible because of its size, but observable none the less because it glowed, was what appeared to be a tiny spec of light. The light hung in the air at about chest height, appeared to be approximately half way down the hallway, and was moving. Patricia quickly looked around the lobby and down the other hallway to discover anything that could have been the source for the tiny light, but everything she could see of her surroundings seemed normal. When she returned her gaze to the light, it seemed to have traveled almost to the end of the hallway, and when it reached the stairway door, it either went out, vanished, or went through it. The light did not look or behave like a reflection. It did not float like dust or some other lighter-than-air debris. Patricia briefly considered that it might have been a flying insect catching the light or even a lightning bug in the building with its fluorescent tail aglow, but the attitude of the movement she observed did not fit those ideas well either. The thing she saw seemed to move at a steady pace without wavering or dipping. The motion of the light as it traveled was more mechanical, to her mind, than organic. The anomaly puzzled Patricia, even made her feel a little uneasy, but new work-related distractions soon refocused her attention, and the strange little light that floated was ultimately forgotten. Patricia admits she had put the event completely out of her mind for years, until another, closer encounter, elevated its significance, and made it part of a story so unique, it is one of her favorite to share when the subject turns to the strange goings on at the mysterious hotel.

Patricia's second encounter with the anomalous light once again took place on the main floor of the hotel. Again, Patricia found herself alone in the early hours of the morning, taking calls and helping the occasional guest at the front desk. It was while she was speaking on the phone that she noticed, with a start, the return of the diminutive floating light. This time the light was halfway down the east hallway, as bright as before and moving in the same slow, deliberate way toward her and the west hallway. Patricia knew instantly that this was the same thing she had seen years ago, there could be no two. Her call ended, Patricia stood in place watching the object slowly come nearer. Patricia saw that at the pace it was traveling, and at that same chest high height, the light would eventually cross directly in front of her, and at close range. Not knowing what exactly she was witnessing or how to react, Patricia remained motionless, her eyes wide, not wanting to blink unless the tiny bead should go out, or perhaps worse, react to her movement. It traveled in the straightest of lines and at a steady pace, almost as if on a string or wire, but there was nothing supporting it, at least nothing visible. The unnatural way it moved, and the confounding fact that it existed at all with no visible source to make or project it, put Patricia on guard. The idea that this might be something beyond the scope of ordinary understanding, one of the hotel's tricks, dictated she continue to stand still and remain silent. With no one else in the vicinity, she would be the sole witness once again. When the light was close enough for Patricia to have her best look at it, she could hardly believe her own eyes. The light was no light at all, but a tiny clear bubble, the approximate size of a pea. As it proceeded across her direct line of vision, she could see its surface, from front, side and back. It was indeed a clear, perfectly round ball of an unknown substance reflecting surrounding light to create the effect of illumination. Patricia knew that this was no ordinary object. An ordinary soap bubble would move erratically as it was carried by its only possible host, a breeze, or other current of air. This was moving in an absolutely straight line, as if resting on some invisible conveyer. Besides, Patricia shared the same space as the object and felt no wind as it went by her, or at any time during the sighting. Patricia was simultaneously amazed and confused, but not quite terrified. She was too intent on observing every detail of what was happening, and still had some faith that an explanation was possible, just not obvious. The incredible scene continued as the tiny bubble retraced its original course down the west hallway, becoming always smaller but no harder to see because the light reflecting off it allowed it to stand out from its surroundings. As she anticipated, the tiny sphere, never changing its pace, traveled to the stairway door and once more disappeared. Patricia stared at the spot on the door for a long time, waiting should the thing reappear. In slow order, she became aware of the ordinary sounds and activity around her, and, as before, duty demanded her return from her temporary, otherworldly fog. She gladly went back to her normal routine, but every time there was a chance to take a break, she occupied her mind with trying to mentally re-create the scene, and to try to explain any part of it in a rational, non-haunted-hotel way. Fearing ridicule, it was months before Patricia volunteered to tell the story to anyone else. When she did, her audiences agreed that her claim was among the most unusual. Years later, she still sometimes tries to work out a plausible explanation, but always, invariably, to no avail.

The facts of the phenomena are few, and simple. Patricia observed, twice, in the same part of an allegedly haunted hotel, a small, pea-sized clear bubble, or ball, traveling in a straight line at a steady pace from her left to her right, arriving at the outer surface of the stairway door, and then going out of view. Thinking "soap" when I hear "bubble," I asked the real "Patricia" if the hotel has a laundry room and was told that they do have a single, large laundry facility located in the subbasement of the building. Even assuming that a soap bubble could survive intact after traveling from two stories below through an air duct, the flight path of the object, as observed by the witness, rules out movement by air current.

The paranormal lexicon includes a popular word for small round flying objects. The gliding ball Patricia describes fits the criteria for an "orb." There is no scientifically satisfactory definition for what an orb is, so we will instead, restrict ourselves to identifying what they look like. In paranormal terminology, an orb is a small, round, usually internally illuminated object that seems to float or fly by virtue of its own power. Unfortunately, many everyday objects appear as orbs on video and in the light from flash photography, so that there is no shortage of mislabeled insects, dander, and digital artifacts polluting the paranormal evidence pool. On the other hand, there exists captured orb phenomena that does not lend itself to easy explanation, and many witnesses that describe encounters with phantom lights that are impossible to explain by merely citing known sources of similar effects.

Almost everything about this particular orb, or bubble, or thing, supports the idea that there was something about it, or the force that acted on it, that was more than just an everyday phenomena subject to misinterpretation. If my source remembers the details correctly, then her tiny bubbles are indeed one of the oddest, most physics defying, and downright goofiest manifestations we have tried to unravel as we continue to scratch our heads and wonder, what else is out there, and why?

As for working in a place like the hotel in my contributor's story, where workmates see phantom employees, fight with the linens, and see clear little balls traversing the hallways, the lady states that she never let the claims, or even her own bizarre observations, dissuade her from putting in her time and doing her job. "I was never really bothered," she said. She represents a section of the population of regular visitors to haunted places that are rarely troubled themselves, and who mostly have to deal with the psychological effects the stories of others can have on their comfort levels at work. For some, weird sights like the sailing bubble might have been enough to chase them out of their positions, or at least put in for a transfer to another part of the building. For others, it seems, paranormal activity can be tolerated, as long as it is not terrifying, or threatening, or, perhaps, small enough to pop.

9
Intruder

As we have seen, possessing the keys to a haunted location, like unpaid overtime or a long commute, can be one of the unexpected unpleasantries attendant to accepting a new situation. It is particularly unsettling when one's line of work is of a kind traditionally expected to be mundane. Short of walking away, which is not always a simple matter, there is little one can do besides bear it until the next opportunity comes into sight, bringing with it an avenue of escape. On the other hand, some professions require their people to be the type that are willing to actively seek trouble out and deal with it, in whatever form it may take. In the early '90s, on New York's Long Island, one such seeker experienced a kind of trouble few learn to deal with very well, in fact, *it* usually deals with *them*.

The young man whose story I present here, we will call John, had spent the last four years of his education studying criminal justice. He did so in between nights waiting tables and days cutting grass, so when his first job after graduation afforded him the title of security officer, it pleased the young man greatly. The student loan payments would start to roll in presently, but now that the property rights exams, and the emergency procedure seminars, and the background checks were all behind him, he did not dwell with gloom upon that obligation. Now that he was taking his first step toward a career in law enforcement, he thought only of how fortunate he was, and of how bright the future would be.

The posting that brought John and his new position together stated that his responsibilities would include, among other things, preforming security patrols of designated areas on foot or in vehicle, investigating and preparing reports on accidents, incidents, and suspicious activities, and sounding the alarm in case of fire or the presence of unauthorized persons. John figured he would eventually be involved in some of those duties once his training was complete and he was authorized to work without a partner. What he couldn't have known was that after only one night of solo patrol he would find himself experienced in all of the above, as well as in a few things radically outside his, or anyone else's, job description.

All newcomers to the security agency John had been accepted by were required to learn their first route by spending time with a veteran officer who would drive the patrol car and spend the rookie's first week going over procedures. John's training mentor was an older gentleman named Oscar who had been in the security business for decades. The patrol route John was asked to learn included two commercial properties and one school.

John learned from his patrol mate that when working with these kinds of establishments, he would occasionally need the assistance of a building representative referred to as the "lock master." Lock masters, it was explained, are typically owners or managers of properties whose duty it is to open buildings should egress or a walk-through become necessary.

Before going out for their first patrol, Oscar informed his charge that theirs was an easy route, and that John would likely find himself in danger of falling asleep on the job before facing any sort of threat from criminal activity. John took some comfort in that, but he felt up to the task of confronting ne'er-do-wells or mischievous kids should the occasion present itself. He wanted to go home safe and sound every night, but also hoped he would gain some experiences on this job to point to when applying for the next step in his career.

During the time the two spent together, Oscar spoke with an easy manner about his past triumphs, close calls, and pet peeves, touching occasionally on details about the job. John was patient with his ride along partner and absorbed what he could, when he could, taking notes between periods of listening politely to his senior's stories. Most of the time John was forced to feign interest, smiling and nodding socially rather than out of genuine interest in the older gentleman's tales. The only time Oscar really got John's attention was the first time they rolled up to the grounds of Sweet Hills Elementary School. "This is it, Johnny Boy," he said, pointing out the window with his thumb toward the long yellow brick building, "Sweet Hills."

John took in the building and its grounds. "What do we do here?" he asked.

"I'll show you," Oscar replied. "But I hope you're not afraid of ghosts." Oscar sat smiling at John waiting for a reaction to his hanging question.

"No," John said, "why?"

"This place is haunted, man," his partner said, craning to briefly look at the building himself before turning his gaze back to John. "I've seen 'em."

Eyeing another one of his partner's storytelling sessions on the horizon, John raised his eyebrows and asked, "What happened?" before discretely closing his notepad and stowing his pen.

Oscar proceeded to recount two ghost stories connected with the school. He started by telling John that, for some reason he did not know, the school building had always had a reputation in the neighborhood for being haunted. Then he told John about an officer

who had been assigned to Sweet Hills years ago, and who had to patrol the halls after receiving a call from base affirming that a security alarm inside the building had been activated. After the arrival of the lock master, the officer entered the premises and began an unaccompanied walk-through of the building. As his story goes, during his patrol, the guard would occasionally hear footsteps in the distance behind him, as if he were being followed. He claimed they sounded softer than his own, which were made in hard soled shoes and were definitely not an echo. When he heard the footsteps, the guard would walk to the center of a hallway, one hand on his container of mace, and then wheel around to catch his pursuer in the act. Each time, however, instead of a confrontation, the footsteps would cease, and he would be faced with the inexplicable sight of an empty hallway. After a few such attempts, the man became frustrated and perturbed. Something definitely did not feel right, but he was not yet ready to abandon the possibility that the sounds were some kind of anomaly created by the environment or, more likely, the work of pranksters inside the building.

Determined to find out, the patrolman decided to go into one of the unlocked classrooms to wait and listen for evidence of someone moving inside the building from there. After hiding in silence for only a short time, he heard the sound of someone walking in soft shoes on the linoleum tiled floor of the hall once again. The sound neared, increasing in volume and traveling directly past the door behind which he hid. Not an echo or a random sound, he thought, but an intruder. Shouting "Hey!" the man pushed the door open and stepped into the hall. Unbelievably, he found himself alone in the utterly empty hallway and immersed in complete silence once again. According to the patrolman, there wasn't enough time for anyone to round the corner, and there was no sound of running from the scene. He could not explain how the sound of the footsteps could have been produced except by human feet. He was at a loss as to their sudden cessation, or the absence of any other sounds before or after them. He strove to make sense of the phenomena. He fought to keep his mind from venturing outside the safe, known causes and effects, but ultimately only one unwelcome explanation fit. He became quite convinced that he was standing in the middle of a haunted location and, shaken, he speedily exited the premises. Later, from the comparative security of his patrol vehicle, the man reported to base that no person was in the building, but that *something* was. As could be expected, his claim that night was met with incredulity and humor and made the man a target for ridicule. The officer refused to return to the interior of the school building that night, or ever again, and had to be reassigned as a result. In spite of years of persistent ribbing, he never budged an inch from his insistence that what he said happened actually did, exactly as he had reported. "That was the first time anybody complained about the school being spooked," Oscar told his young coworker. "The second time, it was me and my partner."

Oscar's personal account began with his admitting to John that he and his former partner had heard of the "haunted" school well before it appeared on their schedule as a part of a new route, but that the men, at that time, put no stock in the claim. During their first week of patrolling the property they joked about its paranormal reputation and particularly about the guard who had been scared off years before. Absolute non-believers, the pair went so far as to make occurrence reports in their logs such as "No ghosts" and "No footsteps," breaking protocol just to ridicule the building's reputation. It was all very light, until the day the two received word that there had been activity detected inside the building by the motion sensors. They arrived before the lock master and so could not enter the building, but they could see several hall lights on inside where only the exit and emergency lights should have been lit. Once out of their vehicle, Oscar and his partner proceeded to test the exterior doors to investigate how a trespasser might have gotten in. All the doors they checked were locked. Either the intruder had a key of his own or he had remained inside the building when the last person exited, locking the doors from the outside. As he was walking back to the front of the building, Oscar said he felt compelled to look up and saw, distinctly, a black figure standing at, and then darting across, the edge of the roof. He called out to his partner that he had seen someone, and told him to go to the ladder stairs leading to the roof on the other side of the building. Oscar raced to the second set of stairs, which were close by on his side. As they climbed toward the roof via the only available means of access, the men shouted for the unauthorized person to stay in place.

Not knowing if there were one or more individuals present, or if they were in any way armed, Oscar peered cautiously over the top edge of the building when he arrived at the top of the stairs. For a moment he observed the flat landscape of the roof by the moonlight and the residual illumination cast by the parking lot lights. He quickly gave the area a visual scan. He could see no obvious signs of trespassers. Then he was momentarily blinded by the beam of his partner's flashlight coming on from the opposite end of the roof and pointing directly at him. Oscar instinctively ducked out of the light, reached for his own flashlight, switched it on, and stood up

shining his beam across the scene. "Security!" Oscar's partner announced, and, in an attempt to coax the intruders into giving up more easily, added untruthfully, "We've already notified police of your presence." As they waited for a response, the two men continued to sweep the rooftop with their flashlight beams in search of any signs of Oscar's intruder.

With one observer at each end of the roof it was possible to see all sides of the few low protrusions that were all that interrupted its flat expanse, as well as the lengths of the low side walls that ran along its perimeter. There was literally nothing in the way of hiding places and no one in sight.

"You see anything?" Oscar shouted.

"Nothing," his partner replied, and after a final, visual sweep of the vacant surface, he added, "You sure you saw someone up here?"

Oscar stepped onto the roof aiming his beam into the two corners on his side and replied, "Definitely." Oscar's partner climbed onto the roof himself and began to walk across it saying, "Well, there's no one up here now."

By then it was obvious to Oscar that whoever he had seen from the ground moments ago was no longer on the roof. He walked to the edge of the building that overlooked the side opposite the street side from which he had observed the figure. He raked the ground with his light for any evidence of his quarry or any disturbance his leaping off the roof to escape might have created in the surrounding brush.

"You think he jumped off?" his partner asked as he joined Oscar at the building's edge.

"You'd break both your legs from this high," Oscar said staring down the twenty foot wall.

They decided to check the grounds from their vantage point on the roof before going back down to wait for the lock master. The men started in opposite directions walking the perimeter of the roof while illuminating the grounds with their lights. They walked slowly and quietly in order not to drown out any sounds from below.

Finally, as they met near one of the metal stairways, Oscar's partner said, "I got nothing."

"Me too," Oscar admitted.

Spreading his arms and shaking his head Oscar added, with a note of disbelief in his voice, "I saw a guy up here. How the hell does a guy get off this roof without us seeing him?"

Before his fellow officer could respond, a car pulled on to the school property, demanding their attention. The lock master had arrived.

The men climbed down the exterior stairs and greeted the new arrival, explaining why he had found them on the roof. As the trio made their way to the school's main entrance, the key holder asked,

"Was it a kid?" The question forced Oscar to consider the appearance of the figure he had seen. Going over the scene in his mind, he began to realize that there was something strange about the suspected trespasser that made describing him difficult. The mental image Oscar had was that of a medium-build male figure with head, torso, arms, and legs down to the knees visible, but all in black. It had the appearance of a silhouette more so than a person observed in the flesh. Oscar could not think of any way the person on the roof could have become so severely backlight, or escaped any highlighting of his features and clothes by the considerable ambient light. He would have to have been clad in a black, light absorbing body suit to produce the effect Oscar had seen. "It was like a dark shadow" was all he could offer by way of description. Later, Oscar would also recall that the figure seemed to dart away extremely quickly from a standstill without producing the sound of running feet against the rooftop or, indeed, any sound at all.

"And when you went up there he was gone?" the lock master asked.

"Yeah. Must have grabbed the ledge and dropped down before we could get up there," Oscar replied, offering the only quasi-credible answer he could think of, but he still did not believe a person would be able to drop from that height without hurting himself badly, or at least compromising himself enough to hinder the rapid disappearance he and his partner were confronted with after racing up to the roof.

"There you are gentlemen," the man said holding the main door open. "I'll be right here when you're ready to leave. I'll keep my eyes open for anyone out here dressed all in black."

"Yeah, and with a nasty limp," Oscar added as he passed the man on his way to patrolling the hallways of Sweet Hills.

After a thorough walk-through of the entire building, checking that each doorknob that should be locked was locked, and looking into the supply closets, cafeteria, and gyms, Oscar and his partner reported back to the lock master.

"Everything's all right," Oscar said. "We turned off the hall lights that were on." Then Oscar asked, "You see or hear anything?"

"No," the man replied, "but how did those lights get turned on? I'm sure they weren't on when the building was locked down."

The lights in the hallways were governed by toggle switches located on the hallway walls and had to be physically flipped to the on or off positions. When Oscar looked to his partner for support, the other man replied, "I have no idea."

Oscar concurred.

Wrapping up his story for John, Oscar said, "You might blame rats for the motion sensor, but rats can't flip a light switch. And that guy I saw didn't jump off the roof and run away without a sound either. He disappeared."

John grinned and asked, "Anything else happen?"

Oscar glanced back at the building and said, "The alarm goes off every now and then, but I never saw or heard anything much after that. Kids like to hang out around here at night. They have all kinds of stories, lights, sounds, but they're all high on something half the time, so who knows?" Oscar put the car in drive and said, "There's something weird about that place though." As the pair headed out to their next location, Oscar added with a laugh, "I don't think it likes us guys in uniform."

John found Oscar's tales amusing, but not outrageous enough to defy explanation. The legend of Sweet Hills was quickly resigned to his mental trash file. The week passed and he finished his time shadowing the veteran confident that he could handle the route by himself.

The following Monday, John received his patrol car keys and prepared himself for his first solo outing. He brought more than enough water and snacks that first night to get him through his shift. He brought along a book to read as well. He felt there would be plenty of time for catching up on some of the ones he had to put off reading while concentrating on his classes. Work like John's affords a person ample downtime for things like reading, and before leaving the company, John would cross many titles off his list, just not on that first night. John's first night would find him otherwise occupied.

It was late September when John began that first week as a full-fledged security officer. His shift began at six o'clock. Darkness, at that time of year on Long Island, came at around seven. Prepared and serious about doing a good job, John made his rounds precisely on schedule and spent extra time inspecting the buildings and grounds of his assigned locations for anything that might be even marginally worth reporting. He enjoyed finally being unsupervised and calling in his reports without his former mentor there to correct or suggest things. Hours passed and John had made his rounds several times without incident before the call came in. Via the walkie-talkie device he was required to wear, the dispatcher at base alerted John to a motion sensor alarm. There was movement detected inside one of his buildings—inside Sweet Hills School. The dispatcher asked him if he was all right dealing with the call on his own. John replied that he would be fine and was on his way. The dispatcher informed John that the lock master for that location was on the way and would meet him there.

Oscar's weird stories were the last thing on John's mind as he drove his vehicle onto the Sweet Hills property. Instead, the young man went over real world scenarios that might explain the alarm, and he steeled himself in preparation for an encounter with flesh and blood vandals or rowdy teens. Upon arrival, the absence of another vehicle in the lot informed John that the lock master had not yet arrived, but someone was inside. Some hall lights were on where a half hour ago, during his drive-by, John had observed those parts of the building in total darkness.

John reported to base that he had arrived, observed lights on in the building, and was exiting his car to check the perimeter of the school. The dispatcher acknowledged John, reminded him to use caution and confirmed that he would be joined by the lock master momentarily. Alert for clues as to the whereabouts of the

trespassers, John walked to the main doors as quietly as he could. When he reached them, he gripped the handles, tugged, and found them immovable. "Maybe an animal," he thought. Then he remembered the lights. A stray lab animal or a trapped bat did not explain the lights being on. John was puzzled because, in any case, the lights didn't make sense. If someone was interested in robbing or vandalizing the classrooms, why would they call attention to their activities by illuminating the halls? Why would they invite investigation? To John, the action seemed either a careless oversight or an arrogant challenge.

John started walking along the east side of the building using his flashlight to look through the darkened classroom windows he passed and checking the exterior doors to make sure they were locked. As he traveled along the perimeter, John listened for voices or other sounds of activity but heard nothing besides the passing cars that were the usual exterior sounds of the location. Once, something in the corner of his eye caused him to shoot a glance up toward the roof, but it must have been a trick of the light because John's flashlight revealed that nothing was there.

Before long John arrived back at the main entrance, but all was not as he had left it. John was surprised to find lights on behind the first pair of doors he had checked, those of the main hallway. He approached them cautiously believing someone might be nearby. Trying the handles, he found the doors had been unlocked giving him access into the school. Apparently the lock master had arrived and found the front of the building abandoned while John had been checking the outside. Now he was not alone, John thought. Now he would be able to perform his duty and the walk-through of the building. He entered and called out a hello that echoed in the long, empty halls. Then a sound, like a desk scraping against the floor somewhere from John's left caused him to turn and start down a lighted hallway. "Hello," he called again, but no answer came in return. Remembering his duties, John began to twist the handles of the doors he passed along the hallway, physically checking that they were locked. The doorknobs twisted slightly, then caught, confirming to John that they were secure. Coming to the end of the hallway, John found and switched on the lights for the next hall to his right. He walked quietly, alert for any sounds, and continued checking all the doors as he went. The hall was long and lined with lockers. Reaching the end of the hallway, John came to an intersection with other dark halls to his right and left. To the right lay the path back to the main entrance. John turned on the lights for the hallway to his left and began a new round of checking doors and keeping his ears open.

There was an uneasy atmosphere developing inside the empty school that John attributed to the fact that places usually associated with noise and activity just seem "wrong" when experienced abandoned. The addition of his apprehension regarding the possible presence of intruders made John more nervous, and he began to feel the need to regularly look behind him to make sure he was actually as alone as he believed himself to be. John wished the lock master would appear or at least respond to his calls. He decided to call out again, if only to ensure he was not mistaken as an intruder by the other man. John turned to face the lighted hall he had just come from. "Hello? Security. Anybody here?" he said. There was no response, but from inside the room he had just passed, John heard something that sounded like tiny bumps or knocks. He walked back and looked inside using his flashlight which confirmed that the room was not only locked and dark, but empty as well. The sounds, whatever they were, must have come from somewhere else, but from where and by what made he could not say.

John continued his walk, and when he reached the end of the hallway he backtracked to the intersection of the two halls. He prepared to switch off the lights behind him and commence his return to the main entrance, but when he reached the intersection he found that the lights in the hallway he had previously checked, and which he had turned on himself, were now turned off.

This could only have happened if someone physically worked the switches. It concerned John that he had not been alert enough to have heard someone acting so close by. John stared down the black hall and called "Hello?" into the darkness, then, with renewed attentiveness, listened for a response. Hearing none, he walked softly toward the light switch panel at the end of the hallway. From halfway up the hall, by the pale illumination reaching the spot through windows in the next hall, he could see that the switches were indeed down. What was less apparent was the answer to the question, by whose hand? John flipped the lights back on, noticing the audible clacking sound they made and wondered why he did not hear at least that sound when he was in the adjacent area. He turned to walk back down the hall when he was halted in his movements by a sight so unexpected, so surreal, that John experienced a brief lightheadedness accompanied by a tingling in his chest.

There, undeniably real in the full light of the hallway fixtures, was the row of doors he had moments ago physically confirmed as locked, now unlocked, and all standing the exact same increment ajar into the hall. Each was two feet or so into the hall at the exact same angle so that each one looked like a mirror image of the other. It was the neat arrangement of the doors that made the sight stranger. It was a tableau accomplished with unnatural speed, at close quarters, and in complete silence. To John, it felt like a deliberate demonstration of stealth and control created to shock him and to let him know that he was dealing with an adversary of superior talents.

Briefly unable to move or utter a word, John struggled to process the scene before him. Had he unconsciously opened the doors when he thought he was checking them, he wondered. But surely, to unlock the doors required a key. Did the kids hiding in the building do this—did the lock master? But he was alone in this part of the building and he heard no sounds of doorknobs, footsteps—anything. It was with that realization that Oscar's accounts of the schools reputation raced to the forefront of John's mind. It was then that his shock began to evolve into fear.

John was conflicted by his impulse to flee and his unwillingness to succumb to hysteria. He noticed he was breathing fast and losing composure. To his great credit, he calmed himself down by breathing deeply and turning his fear into something he could use, into anger. He did not care to be frightened out of his first job, or to be pranked by anyone, not even a ghost. John was also determined not to allow the lock master to report to everyone that he had run out of the haunted school like the infamous coward before him. John's sense of duty dictated that he should, must, recheck each room, relock the doors, put out the lights and report the incident. "Whatever is going on here," John thought, "it is now my job to observe and record it."

Satisfied at least that, at present, there was no danger, John took a quick look into each room as he turned the doorknob switches back to their locked positions and shut the doors one by one. He worked fast and shot glances left and right as he went from door to door to shake an uncomfortable feeling of being watched. When he reached the end of the hallway, he turned off the lights he had left on in the east wing and walked resolutely, if hurriedly, to the end of the hallway with the doors that opened by themselves, and put out those lights as well. He did not dare look back on his way out to see if there had been any sudden, inexplicable change in the scenery. Two left turns later he was approaching the main doors. Before taking the last few steps through the main entrance, John halted, thinking that he did not want to leave the lock master, if he was still in the building, in total darkness. Before reaching for the last bank of light switches, he turned and called, "Is anybody here? I'm leaving." As if in response, John received a blast of static on the walkie-talkie that hung on his belt. It startled him because it was unexpected, but also because it was strange. The sound was not like any transmission or interference he had heard before. There was a unique quality to the rush of hisses and crunches that blasted over the miniature speaker. It might have been scrambled words, but the tone was unfamiliar—aggressive. No matter its nature or origin, John considered the transmission a sign that it was time to end the investigation, and he left the building. Outside, he turned to watch the main door slowly close behind him, separating him from the inhospitable void inside with a hard click. That metallic snap seemed to be the final installment in a series of covert statements that together stated, "Now you know. Stay out."

Outside, John had time to regroup and consider the odd events of the evening and how he would go about relating them to his coworkers at base. John decided there would be no value in embellishing his report with his personal feelings about what he had experienced and to omit the episode with the opening doors altogether. After all, they were all re-secured, no longer an issue, and, at any rate,

impossible to explain. The random sounds and the light switches he attributed to the lock master. The ill-timed, weird static must have been picked up from a source in the area, perhaps even a walkie-talkie being carried by the lock master. There would be no need to mention that either.

Back inside the car, John called base and reported that he had inspected the building, had found lights on but no one inside. He made the dispatcher aware that he had checked all doors in the hallways with lights on, that they were all secure, and that he had extinguished all lights on his way back out. "How'd you get in?" the dispatcher asked.

John replied, "The lock master unlocked the entrance doors when I was around back. I don't know where he is now. He might still be in the building."

"That's not possible," the dispatcher said. "I just got off the phone with him. The guy said he can't find his keys and he's going to be late."

John looked over at the building, saw that it was still dark, and then scanned the parking area for another vehicle. He was alone, and had been from the beginning. John informed the dispatcher that he would wait for the lock master.

"Where will you be?" he was asked.

"In my vehicle," John replied before signing off and rubbing his closed eyes in an effort to erase the image of the neatly opened doors and the imagined entity that displayed them for him.

A half hour later, John and the lock master inspected the front door. It was locked. With all quiet and the light situation resolved, the men parted ways, one returning home for a little more TV before retiring for the night, and the other to finish his rounds and to contemplate his future as the nighttime steward of a haunted school.

John decided to continue his visits to Sweet Hills, opting to check the exterior of the premises by surveilling from his patrol vehicle, and to keep his past and any future strange experiences there to himself. He adopted a "do what you have to do" attitude about his duties there, but admitted that an escalation in activity would probably have pushed him to his limit. He processed the anomalous occurrences of that night by clinging to the fact that, although outside his ken and far afield of his comfort zone, the happenings at Sweet Hills were not, in his eyes, proof positive of the paranormal, and that he was never in real danger. The ultimate comfort came in the fact that he never was called to go back inside the peculiar school with the wayward doors, and the foot-less footsteps, and the rooftop shadow man. After that first encounter, the building was quiet until the day John's next route went into effect and he was rid of Sweet Hills School. As the years passed, John kept his impressions to himself, but also kept an eye on the new hires who were typically given that first, "easy," route. Whenever present, he would watch their eyes as they returned and recapped their nightly duties for traces of a faraway stare, or an involuntary glance down at the floor at certain words. He would not initiate a conversation, but would be there should they appear to need to talk to someone who understood what it felt like to have your sense of reality shaken up a bit, or to feel watched and unwanted in a supposedly empty space. He would listen and understand should someone returning from Sweet Hills need to talk to another who knew what it was to feel like an unwelcome guest—like an intruder.

10
Inside

As was recounted in the opening chapter, my experience with the phantom footsteps, while house hunting with our real estate agent years ago, was the catalyst that started me thinking about the extraordinary phenomena some people encounter, not accidentally, or intentionally, but as an unsolicited part of their daily lives. The whole crux of my inquiries and the exercise of this book was to examine how people of different stripes manage the challenge of being in that uniquely uncomfortable position. I was interested to see if there were any patterns to learn from or any universal advice to be had that might aid other individuals struggling to cope, and forearm more who one day might find themselves in like situations.

As the process of gathering information progressed, I realized that I had been put in a position to do myself and you, dear reader, a definite service. What better way to conclude this collection of stories than to put myself, and consequently myself as a proxy for you, into the very situation I endeavored to learn more about. In a weird way I had inadvertently joined the ranks of those compelled by their professions to enter paranormally active locations. As a writer, am I not obliged to research my subject from all sides, including the inside?

I decided I would become a surrogate key holder, and, with full knowledge of its reputation, enter and spend time in one of these active locations myself. I would record the experience, and report what happened there to you from the viewpoint of an insider. For my proving ground I chose the fabled Haldeman Mansion. It was within reach and Lora Shirey, the director of paranormal affairs there, kindly consented to open the house and outbuildings to me for exclusive use. We selected a date convenient for both myself and the activities slated for the mansion, and devised a plan for receiving and returning the keys. By that time I had heard many accounts of people who dealt with re-entering haunted locations over periods of days, weeks and even years. I had only to return for one evening to my borrowed haunted house, but that would be enough to sample the experience. Lora's history at the mansion was enough to seal the buildings reputation, but in addition to her tale I had heard many other stories about bizarre happenings witnessed by guests and investigators at that site. What awaited me, I did not know. After hanging up with Lora, I circled the date on my calendar. In one week I would be inside a potential paranormal funhouse—and alone.

As a layperson, as opposed to a committed paranormal investigator, I never understood or cared for the idea of investigating locations in the dark. People who ask for the ghost hunter's help usually describe their experiences as happening during the daytime hours, or if at night, by the illumination of their indoor lighting. If doors open and shut by themselves, or if objects move or fly off ledges and shelves, I would want to see that clearly and right away, as well as as much of the surrounding environment as possible for clues as to the causes. Also, buildings, abandoned or occupied, are often the domains of humans by day and critters by night. If a cat moves the hem of a curtain or a mouse disturbs items in the kitchen, I would want to know that right away. So for my fact finding vigil I decided to ask for the house during early evening hours when the sun was still flooding through the windows and I would have a clear view of the room I was in, the ones adjacent, and the rest of the space as far as the eye could see. Also, photographic images would be clear and of good quality in the full sunlight should I be able to capture anything with my camera.

My method for substituting myself as an employee in a haunted location and observing the effects of my strange venue would be simple, I would occupy each room, from the attic to the basement, alone and in complete silence for an equal amount of time until I had covered the entire building. I would have with me a pad and pen for taking notes, use the clock function on my phone to record times and durations, and run a digital recorder for the entire length of time spent in each room to capture audio phenomena, audible or otherwise. A camera would also be nearby. My silence would ensure that I did not corrupt any precious audio as well as prevent me from creating an aura of expectation by asking for things to happen and then being able to misinterpret random sounds as the anticipated responses. I would simply write down anything seen, heard, or felt and note the time for later reference. An allowance for gasps of horror represented the sole exception to my rule.

The week passed quickly, and soon I found myself preparing to walk into the haunted Haldeman Mansion.

At the time of my entrance into the building, I am opened minded about, but naturally unable to confirm the nature of the strange things that are happening to people in places like Haldeman. I believe there is something going on around us, perhaps more so in places like the one I am about to camp in, but I don't believe we can yet claim to know exactly what it is. I believe that the people who relate their ghost stories to me are telling the truth, but not having witnessed the phenomena myself, I cannot honestly adopt their conviction. After my first visit to the mansion, I recorded a sound that was not audible to me or others present and that I cannot, so far, satisfactorily interpret as anything less than a disembodied voice. That is evidence of something that is not easily explained. With that item captured and confirmed, and with all I have heard about the location keeping a respectful distance but nonetheless palpable presence in the back of my mind, I step inside, and close the door behind me.

Lora advised me to start rolling my digital recorder as soon as I entered the house because the voices are believed to be particularly active when someone first comes in from outside. I had the device on and running in my hand as I walked into the first room. The house, having no window treatments to block the sun, was full of light that completely illuminated the rooms. Inside it was still and my footsteps, as they scraped across the old, uneven floors, were eerily amplified by that stillness. The emptiness inside tossed the sounds from wall to wall, and void to void until they ebbed, restoring the customary heavy silence of the house. Every sound I would make the rest of the evening would seem like a disturbance. I halted in the middle of the space and listened for any internal sounds. As this was my first experience re-entering a bona fide haunted location, I stood in place and scanned the areas in my sightline for a long while, unsure of what to expect, or even if I should expect anything to happen. All was still. I put the recorder on the soft leather cover of my notepad to eliminate any noise that might be created by the movement of my fingers as I held it. I put the notepad down in the middle of the floor and stepped back to the rear wall to have the widest view of the room, and waited.

There is something odd about being alone in an old, decaying house at the best of times. Add the preconception that strange things happen to people who enter there and you have the potential for some genuine apprehension. I could understand how board members and volunteers might prefer working here in twos. As for myself, I was on the alert but calm. As I observed and listened, I began to dwell on the typical types of spirit manifestations experienced people describe, and attempted to prepare myself for different kinds of supernatural activity by visualizing them. I thought that by doing this I might be less startled should the real thing happen because I would have already dealt with it once in my mind. What, I asked myself, picking a corner of the room, if that door opened by itself? What if footsteps came across the floor and stopped where I was standing? How would I feel if a voice came from somewhere upstairs, or if an invisible hand touched my shoulder? In my mind, I am pleased to report, I saw myself reacting with intense fascination but without fear. I reasoned that I wouldn't be alarmed if a living person did any of those things. Ghosts, if they are anything, are basically people, so why be overly alarmed if they do something similar. Once you get accustomed to the concept of their altered state, you are essentially sharing space with a brother, I reasoned again, this time adding a healthy dash of hope. The room I was in was quiet with no detectable vibe or hint of peculiarity. Becoming comfortable with the silence and the isolation, and satisfied that I had given this first stop on my tour its due, I picked up my gear and moved on to the next room.

Now I was in the Haldeman Mansion ballroom. This room is wider than the others in the house and has two fireplaces instead of one, but it is hardly what comes to most people's minds at the mention of the word "ballroom." Preservation Society events are held here, accounting for the incongruous modern tables and chairs scattered about. I was told a reenactor will pretend to be one of the Mrs. Haldemans of yore at a tea event here in a few weeks to raise funds in aid of the renovation of the building. A ghost of sorts, I mused as I stood picturing the scene. I put the notepad and recorder down on one of the tables and took a seat in a chair. This is the area where the spirit of Henry Haldeman is supposed to breathe hard in visitor's ears in order to make himself known or scare them away. It was here that I captured the EVP of exactly that sound months ago. I am alert for that or any other sound as I lean forward in my chair. I scan the room and the rooms on either side for movement, a shadow, anything. This evening there is an abundance of birdsong outside. The leafy outer limbs of the trees that house those birds rustle gently in an almost constant breeze. For the next ten minutes, those soothing sounds are all that can be heard. I wondered if my recorder was having more success than I was as I rose and moved again, this time to the artifact room.

If you have been following paranormal investigative culture, you will have heard of numerous theories that attempt to shed light on the why, where, and how of all types of fantastic phenomena. Although future science might one day find merit in some or all of them, today they are mostly interesting ideas, and circumstantial at best. One of these thoughts is that, besides structures and land, objects can trigger or even house paranormal energy left there by previous owners or events. With this concept in mind I slowly walked the Haldeman artifact room, passing my hand over original pieces of furniture and reading descriptive placards. In addition to the few Victorian sofas and framed paper memorabilia in the room, there sits a long, glass-fronted display case. Exhibited inside are a collection of Native American stone items, pottery shards, and small examples of items from nature collected and used by Sammuel Haldeman during his time as a student and professor. With all these items unearthed and valued by a man whose spirit is purported to haunt the premises surrounding me, I hoped for improved odds on experiencing some of the mansion's ghostly activity. For the next ten minutes I sat noiselessly scanning the areas in my field of vision, ready and waiting for anything. While I passed time in my chair I remembered another part of the lore of Haldeman Mansion. There is a belief that sensitive people experience headaches after spending time in the artifact room, headaches that evaporate the moment sufferers walk back over the thresholds leading in and out. After ten minutes I notice no such sensation, and not having witnessed anything else, I move myself and my gear again, this time to the bottom of the main staircase. My next stop, after a ten minute rest seated on the lower steps, would be the second story and the personal living quarters of everyone who ever lived in the house, and perhaps of a few who un-live in them now.

As my investigation by silent daytime vigil proceeded from room to room, I continued to run my digital recorder, always placing it on top of the cushioned cover of my notebook to reduce the effect of vibrations caused by my movements, and always on the floor in a central part of the room I was in. The only sounds I made were those of occasional footsteps and those associated with getting in and out of chairs, or off ledges or steps as I moved to experience different parts of the house. The only time I spoke was to identify sounds that might have been picked up by the device that I wanted to document as *not* being paranormal. If a sound or voice from outside was loud enough to be heard inside, I would say out loud, "That was outside." If I bumped something or moved an object in the room, I would say, "That was me." Anything present on the recording not so identified would be potential evidence of a paranormal audio event.

As the evening progressed, I continued my supervision of Haldeman Mansion in the shells of the former bedrooms upstairs.

I kept watch in the "room with the fireplace," the "room with the red trim," the "crooked room," and even from inside the lone closet in the house because it was told to me that spirits can sometimes be encountered there. I listened and watched, but nothing disturbed the almost anomalous calm of the house reputed to be so active when others come to visit. Having observed all the rooms on the second floor at least once, there were only two locations left, the attic and the basement. I doubt anyone would argue that attics and basements are the least comfortable places in any dwelling even under the best of circumstances. The confining nature of each, especially in very old buildings like this one, the limited lighting, and the general atmosphere of bleakness, combine to inspire quick exits. Imagine sitting in the middle of either alone in a haunted house and you will understand my experiencing the first faint pangs of trepidation of the evening as I entered first one, and then the other.

I was told that if I spent time in the attic, I should keep my ears open for young voices as the children purported to still be present at the mansion frequent that lonely spot. I kept them opened, as I moved around the cramped space as quietly as possible getting the lay of the room and settling on a spot from which to observe. My recorder was placed on a central part of the floor and I stationed myself near the window where I could see most of the area and also notice if any sound-contaminating activity was going on outside. For ten minutes I stared from spot to spot steeled for any phenomenon the house might have in store. In the attic I was more vulnerable than anywhere else because there was only one way out and that was not available by a clear and opened path. Ten minutes ticked away. Perhaps to the detriment of my experience, but accepted graciously by me, no cause for alarm manifested during my time beneath the rafters. My next and final stop, the basement, would be the mansion's last chance to make me a believer. I gathered my things and headed down.

There are several opinions regarding the timing and frequency of paranormal activity. Some say that it is fickle, occurring randomly at some times and not at all at others. Some believe a certain degree of sensitivity is required to experience paranormal events. Yet others hypothesize that the authors of paranormal events choose the living people they wish to connect with and reject others. We might never know what really governs this mysterious category of phenomena, but whatever laws or prerequisites or favors it fancied on the evening in question, it seemed that they were not, so far, jelling for me.

The basement of the Haldeman Mansion is a small collection of dark, damp, rooms with dirt floors. During my visit there a dehumidifier was running loudly in the middle one. The sound of the machine contaminated the recording environment, but I kept the digital device going because when dealing with things we cannot explain, we must allow for results beyond those we expect. Like the attic before it, the basement was a spot with only one way in or out. Walking to the area farthest from the stairs put me in the somewhat uneasy position of being susceptible to the shock of a paranormal event or a ghostly prank with no option but to remain in place until it passed, and then to retreat with that awful, imagined clutching feeling at my back. Of all the parts of the house I had occupied that evening, the basement was the only one I felt eager to get out of. That was probably the result of the effect of being cut off from the light and the view of the familiar world just outside a window. It could also be that I was mentally ready to leave after almost two hours of probing the house. The possibility also exists that there was something else inspiring me to remove myself from the premises. After only five minutes I am heard on the recording saying "All right" indicating that I had had enough of the close environment below the rest of the house, then there is the sound of the dehumidifier getting louder as I passed it, and then my footsteps climbing back up the wooden stairs to the main level, and the light.

After experiencing the basement, my silent investigation was officially complete. I had given any forces present ample opportunity to have their way with me, but had not been faced with apparitions, or accosted by disembodied voices, or touched by transparent hands all evening. The sun was lower in the sky and soon it would be dark. I was ready to leave, but decided to perform a final experiment before relinquishing my private access to the house. As an experiment to see if it made any difference, I would go back upstairs and walk through the rooms one last time, but this time I would speak out loud, as if to the presences there in an attempt to provoke responses.

After arriving at the second floor and its crumbling bedchambers once more I said, "I am going to ask a few questions in this empty house where nothing has happened and where no one is except me,

to see if it changes what comes out on my recorder." Then I asked, "If there is anyone here in this house with me, I would like to know, before I leave, if you are here." I waited a moment and then began to walk through the rooms on my way back to the stairs. "I have spent some time here. Now I am leaving," I said holding the recording device in front of me as I went. Believing it would be appropriate to identify myself, I added, "My name is John. I am leaving now." After another waiting period, I turned and descended the stairs to the first floor.

I walked from the hall to the artifact room, then paused announcing, "If there is anybody here and you want me to stay longer, I'll stay." I stood silently to allow my recorder to detect any response cleanly, then said, "If there are people here and you want me to leave, I'm leaving right now." After a pause, and satisfied that

I had done all I could in the house that evening, I exited Haldeman Mansion. Back outside, I took a last look at the building, making sure to inspect all the windows lest a teasing figure be staring out from one. One was not.

I still had the Summer Kitchen at my disposal, the out building where Lora Shirey had had her most terrifying encounter to date. I entered that building and spent time first in the small loft and then in the main room with the large fireplace below. After sitting and recording in both places in silence, I again used my final minutes to speak out loud for the sake of the comparison of results. Once, I thought I heard people outside. If anyone was there, by the time I walked to the door, opened it and looked over the area, which was a matter of seconds, no one was in sight.

Finally, it was time to find Lora and thank her for her, and the society's generosity. When she asked me if anything unusual had happened, I told her that I would only know that for sure after reviewing my digital recordings. As far as any spectacular encounters were concerned, I admitted that on this particular evening, for me, all was quiet inside the mansion.

On the ride home, I played back some of the tracks I had recorded. I held the speaker on the device close to my ear in order to hear details over the drone of the car's engine. The sound quality was poor and, by the time I arrived home, I had heard nothing worth rewinding to to hear a second time.

My time as a returnee to a haunted location was over. It is the consensus among veterans that the odd occurrences known popularly as paranormal phenomena are prone to randomness. People I interviewed agreed that sometimes the activity is high and sometimes it is nonexistent. Perhaps circumstances simply did not line up for me. Researching from the inside had been a valuable experience and had produced observations worthy of commentary, but how much more compelling it would it have been, I thought as that night ended, if only there had been evidence.

For weeks I left the writing of my account on the back burner. From time to time I thought about how best to make the uneventful story as interesting as possible in light of the fact that there was no paranormal activity available to serve as a highlight. In fact, it had been so long between my time at Haldeman and the time I decided to put the account on paper, that I had already forgotten details regarding the sequence of rooms visited, the sounds outside, etc. It was time to revisit that evening by listening to the digital recordings I made and taking notes. Because I found the playback quality so poor the first time I listened to portions of the tracks, I employed high definition headphones for the job of listening to them a second time. That upgrade was a game changer. What I heard then was so strange, so unexpected, that I had to listen to clips over and over again to make sure I was actually hearing what I believed I was.

The result of that session was the discovery of an abundance of sounds and voices that should not have been on the recordings, but somehow were. Either Haldeman Mansion is situated at the center of an unusual electronic anomaly producing crossroads, or it is inhabited by sound-producing things I could neither see nor hear with my eyes and ears. There are so many instances of sounds without origin, that I must edit the results in order not to make my report too long! The following is an abbreviated inventory of sounds and words captured during my unaccompanied, silent vigil in that vacant house.

During my first walk-through of the ballroom there is a sigh, or breath, audible on the recording. This is the exact phenomena Lora said happened regularly in that room, and is similar to the sound I recorded there on my first visit. One minute and ten seconds later another sound is heard. It is vocal in quality and sing-song in cadence. It is impossible to concretely identify or interpret, but it is there and I did not hear it in real time. Two tracks later, in the upstairs room nicknamed the "room with red trim," a very loud breath is recorded, as if someone stood, or was laying down as the recorder was always on the ground, inches from the microphone and breathed harshly into it. Again, I heard no such sounds at the time and I assure you I did not blast any breaths into the recorder then or at any other time during my investigation. What follows four seconds later is stranger still. After the loud breath a child's voice is heard. I hear three words and believe I can discern what they are, but in the interest of remaining impartial, I will keep my interpretation to myself and be satisfied reporting solely the capture of this sound.

Shortly after, in the next room, there is a small breath followed by a short vocal sound recorded as I stood in the upstairs closet. There is a hollow, unnatural quality about this breath, and all the others, in that they almost sound superimposed over the recordings of the ambient sounds. Their resonance and decay don't seem to comply with the environmental conditions affecting the room tone, the sounds of my movements, and the noises outside. When I kept watch in the attic, I heard no internal sounds. Nothing audible reached my ears, but apparently a machine does not have to be particularly "sensitive." There were several sighing sounds recorded during my time on the topmost level with the most impressive coming at the end. Just before and during the time I moved my notepad and recorder from the attic floor, there are two little puffing sounds followed by a harsh exhale very close to the mic. I heard nothing in real time, and never held the recorder up to my face.

On the downstairs landing, where I camped for five minutes, there are more faint breaths or sighs. There are so many of these that I later asked for back-up listeners to review them to confirm that the sounds were not all coming from *me*. I began to doubt that there could be so many of these sounds in so many parts of the house without them coming from a consistent source, one that went where the recorder went. The only logical conclusion was that I was unknowingly sighing and breathing into the device myself. The other listeners, both of whom are familiar with the characteristics of my voice, concurred in their opinions that what they were hearing was not normal, and not me. If I was not the source of the sighs and the breaths traveling wherever the recorder went, what was?

At four minutes and eleven seconds into my recording made on the first floor landing, I capture a voice. This voice is what I would describe as a hard whisper and it says, phonetically, "Ah-lay-ah-poo." This odd sounding word, or phrase, or name, is gibberish to me, but it is there, an undeniably human voice recorded in the absence of other human beings.

My notes go on to list more sighs, breaths, harsh breaths and miscellaneous odd vocal sounds in the rooms upstairs and down.

A child's voice sounds a second time near a cupboard under the stairs on the first floor. I believe I can discern the last two words, but suffice it to say there is someone's voice present on the recording where no one's voice should be.

In the basement, where I noted that the general feeling was different, there is recorded a definite vocal moan or grunt as I am going back up the stairs. What it is or what made it, I do not know, but it wasn't me and I did not hear it although it is loud enough on the recording that I should have.

Perhaps the unexplained sound most relevant to my visit to Haldeman Mansion came at three minutes and six seconds into my final track recorded in the house. This was during the time I experimented with speaking out loud, as if to any intelligence present. I am heard saying, "Hi, my name is John. I'm going to be leaving now." Eight seconds later a low voice is heard saying what sounds like "J. . . John." All that would be enough to make anyone wonder what is going on in the old mansion by the river, but there is yet more weirdness to report. In the kitchen/smokehouse, I put the recorder down on a small table while engaged in tidying an antique straw bed there that had sagged to the floor. On the recording you hear me rustling the mattress. To do this I had to turn my back to the recorder. That is why it is particularly hard to explain the extended recording of breathing and wheezing close to the microphone that is captured at this time. Approximately three minutes later, breaking the long silence, there is another, in fact the last, of the sighing breaths complete with its customary deviance from the audio qualities of the other "normal" sounds on the track.

Finally, after eight-and-a-half minutes spent in the building and my experiment at an end, I am heard saying, "Some people say things have happened here, but I'm in an empty house—I'm in an empty room. I don't hear anything, I don't see anything, I don't feel anything. To me this is a vacant building with nothing and nobody inside." After a pause I add, "It's pretty foolish to be talking to an empty building, so I am going to stop. I'm going to leave." After a final pause I am heard moving, gathering things, and walking to the door. Seconds later there is an odd sound. It is a brief, two-note buzzy sound an indeterminate distance from the recorder. It is impossible to identify, but it has some of the "off" quality of the other EVPs. The timing might suggest a parting shot from the other side to the paranormally deaf interloper making his way out the door. At eight minutes and fifty-nine seconds the recording, and my foray into paranormal research, ends.

What those recorded sounds and voices are, I do not know. How they came to be on the digital tracks, I also do not know. Some of the theories that attempt to explain these phantom voices suggest that they are those of human beings in an altered state, or spirit voices, or alternately, that they are fragments of transmissions from CB radios, cell phones, or baby monitors. Both offer explanations that are difficult to accept. With no information regarding their source and no visual confirmation of a person or spirit in the vicinity, we can only say that the voices are sounds of unknown origin that fit our idea of what spirit voices sound like. Similarly, we cannot verify that CB or baby monitor users were broadcasting their voices at the times the recordings were imprinted. Also, I find it highly uncharacteristic of users of those, and other electronic devices, that they should be sighing and moaning and exhaling into their apparatus. Excerpts from any of those sources should consist of pieces of normal conversations. Another inconsistency is the fact that there were no anomalous imprints on tracks recorded when I used the same device around my home and on location during interviews, only at the mansion. In those instances I used the device in more densely populated areas where one could expect interference. In contrast, the mansion has a river on one side and other abandoned buildings on the other.

When I entered Haldeman Mansion, it was with prior knowledge of its reputation. Now, knowing what I do regarding the sounds recorded there, I admit that I would be more wary about spending additional time there alone. It has given me an enhanced appreciation for the people who face like challenges day in and day out.

The basic definition of the word haunted, as it refers to locations, is the state of being occupied by spirits. Based on my brief time as a key holder, I cannot go that far in describing the place I temporarily occupied, but it is obvious that things happen there, and in our world generally, that have yet to be defined. Consider that before the year 1543, anyone disputing the notion that the sun orbits the Earth would have been roundly ridiculed by the scientific community and labeled a fool by their peers. Before committing to the notion that there can be no altered states of human existence, and that there can be no intersection of one plane of existence with another, reflect on the fact that that community and those peers of yesteryear could not have been more wrong, and that anyone adhering to their beliefs today is considered a fool.

To human beings, the world is vast. We can see much of it, but we cannot see to the end of it. With that in mind, perhaps the most moderate approach to assembling a perception of the natural world is to believe what you genuinely feel is true, but to not claim to know what you cannot prove, and to challenge what does not fit your perspective on reality, but to not condemn what you cannot disprove.

Although there are definitely those among us who are hysterical, excitable, ignorant, dishonest, or of disordered minds, the majority of people you will meet will be of the perfectly normal variety. They see what their eyes fall upon and hear what their ears receive. Sometimes, in the places we call haunted, things happen that we can only observe and ponder. I know, not only because I have had the privilege of the confidence of honest people, but because now it has happened to me.

Perhaps someday, even someday soon, it will be your turn.

Add Your Voice

Your contribution is key!

If you have had paranormal encounters in the course of
your professional pursuits and would like to share them, please
submit your story to skeletonkeysstories@gmail.com.
Contributions are appreciated and will be considered for future
volumes of *Skelton Keys*. The author thanks all prospective
contributors and assures them that all materials will be taken
seriously and treated with respect.

Thank you.